St. John
On Foot and By Car

St. John
On Foot and By Car

A Walking and Motor Guide
to the History and Natural Beauty of
St. John, U.S. Virgin Islands

Salt Pond Coral Art

By Randall and Rebecca Koladis

Copyright © 2021 My Island Ways, Inc.
All Rights Reserved

Library of Congress Control Number: 2020905380
ISBN 978-0-9708919-1-4

Third Edition

Literary Editor: Nick Nobbe
Researcher: Rachel Star Koladis
Photo Editor: Joshua Seaward Koladis
Graphics Arts: Aquastone Graphic Arts & Print, Hartford, CT
Printed By: Hadley Printing Company, Inc., Holyoke, MA

MY ISLAND WAYS, INC.,
a nonprofit corporation,
P.O. Box 270031, West Hartford, CT 06117
P.O. Box 8340, St. John USVI 00830

For Randy's sister Darien with whom the authors enjoyed many treasured moments in the Virgin Islands

"Memory Eternal"

Contents

St. John and the Guidebook
Welcome to St. John......11-13
Getting Around......13-14
About Our Guidebook......14-15
Local Customs and Useful Tips......15

History ■
Early Visitors, Inhabitants, and Colonization......17-21
Enslaved Labor Trade......21-24
Life as an Enslaved Laborer......24
Revolt of 1733......25-28
Transition from Colonization......28-32
Creation of the Virgin Islands National Park......32-36
    Laurance S. Rockefeller, Frank Stick,
    Harold Hubler, Archie Alexander

Walking Tour of Cruz Bay ■
Brief History of the Town......37-39
Start of Walking Tour......39-40
Story of Lind Point Battery......40
Friends of the National Park......40-42
Administration ("Battery") Building......42-44
Franklin A. Powell, Sr. Park......44-45
Nazareth Lutheran Church......45-46
St. John Development Corporation:
    Theovald E. Moorehead, Julius E. Sprauve, Sr.,
    Albert Sewer, Ronald A. Morrisette, Sr., Loreden Boynes, Sr....46-48
More Notable Locals
    Carl Francis......49, 78
    Doris and Ivan Jadan......49-51
    Miss Lucy......52
    Guy Benjamin......52-53
    Julius E. Sprauve, Sr.......47, 53-54
Coconut Coast/Frank Bay......55-57
Martin–van Beverhoudt Family Plot......57-58
Local Cuisine......58-59
Carnival......59-60
Elaine Sprauve Library......61-62

North Shore Motor Tour

Caneel Bay Plantation...63-64
Gibney-Oppenheimer Families and Beach...............................65-67
"Easter Rock" and Peace Hill..67-68
Trunk Bay Beach/Boulon Family Guest House.........................68-71
Cinnamon Bay...71-72
Maho Bay Beach/Camps/Stanley Selengut.............................72-73
Annaberg School/Colonial Education.......................................73-75
Annaberg Sugar Works..75-78
   *History of Key Ownerships: Isaac Constantin, Salomon Zeeger,
   James E. Murphy, Mary Murphy Sheen, Hans Berg,
   Abraham C. Hill, George E. Francis, Antoine Anduze,
   Carl E. Francis, Herman O. Creque, Jackson Hole Preserve/
   National Park*
Francis Bay Ruins/Ethel McCully...79-82

Centerline Motor Tour to East End and South Shore

Bethany Moravian Church..84-85
Adrian Plantation...86-87
Estate Catherineberg...87-89
Coral Bay..89-91
Emmaus Moravian Church...91-92
East End Profile/Basketmaking...93-95
East End Sightseeing...95-102
East End School..95-96
Carolina Corral..96
St. John Donkeys..96-97
Fort Frederiksvaern ("Fortsberg") and British Battery.............98-100
Privateer Bay/Pirates...100-102
Coral Bay Organic Farm...102
Greg "Paz" Myers..103-104
Salt Pond Bay...104-106
Little Lameshur Bay...106-107
Bay Rum Still and Bay Oil Business...107
Story of Countess Daisy...107-111
Tektite Mission..111-112

Map of St. John...114-115

CONTENTS 9

Hiking Trails ▪

North Shore
(1) Lind Point Trail 116-117
(2) Caneel Hill Trail 117-118
(3) Caneel Hill Spur Trail 118
(4) Peace Hill Trail 118
(5) Cinnamon Bay Loop Trail, NPS, Self-Guided 118-126
(6) Cinnamon Bay Trail 126
(7) Francis Bay Trail 126
(8) Annaberg School Trail 127
(9) Annaberg Sugar Works, NPS Self-Guided 127-136
(10) Leinster Bay Trail 136
(11) Johnny Horn Trail 137
(12) Brown Bay Trail 138-139

South Shore
(13) Salt Pond Bay Trail 139
(14) Drunk Bay Trail 139
(15) Ram Head Trail 139
(16) Tektite Trail 140
(17) Yawzi Point Trail 141
(18) Bordeaux Mountain Trail and
(19) Bordeaux Peak Spur Trail 141
(20) Lameshur Bay Trail 141

Centerline
(21) L'Esperance Trail 142-145
(22) Reef Bay Trail, NPS, Self-Guided 145-157
(23) Great Sieben Trail 157-158

Beaches ▪

North Shore
(1) Honeymoon Beach 159-160
(2) Caneel Bay Resort Beach 160
(3) Hawksnest Beach 161
(4) Gibney-Oppenheimer Beach 161
(5) Jumbie Beach 161-162
(6) Trunk Bay Beach 162-163
(7) Cinnamon Bay Beach 163
(8) Maho Bay Beach 164
(9) Francis Bay Beach 164-165

(10) Leinster/Waterlemon Cay Beach 166

East End
(11) Brown Bay Beach 166
(12) Haulover Beach 167
(13) Hansen Bay Beach and
(14) Saltwell Bottom Beach 167
South Shore
(15) Salt Pond Bay Beach 167-168
(16) Little Lameshur Beach 168-169
(17) Genti Bay Beach 169
(18) Westin Resort Beach 169-170

**Checklist of Mammals, Reptiles, Amphibians,
and Arthropods** 171-178

Checklist of Birds 179-184

Checklist of Corals, Fish, and Marine Life
Corals 185-187
Fish and Marine Life 188-196

Checklist of Trees, Plants, and Cacti
Common Trees 197-209
Flowering Plants 209-211
Thorny, Spiny Cacti, and Other Plants 212-217

Sources and Credits 219-222

Special Thanks 222-223

About the Authors .... Inside Back Cover

St. John and the Guidebook

Welcome to the Island

St. John is part of the Virgin Islands, a 60-mile archipelago of volcanic-formed islands in the eastern reaches of the Greater Antilles.

Peter Fitzgerald, Courtesy Wikitravel under creative commons license, layout modifications (added "U.S. Virgin Islands" and altered distances between islands), https://wikitravel.org/shared/File:US_Virgin_Islands_regions_map.png

On one side of the chain is the Atlantic; on the other, the Caribbean. The cluster is divided into two groups—the U.S. Virgin Islands

(USVI) and the British Virgin Islands (BVI). The U.S. group includes 68 islands in total and measures 133 square miles. The largest U.S. islands are St. Croix, followed by St. Thomas and St. John, the latter measuring just 21 square miles. The British Virgin Islands consist of four principal islands—Tortola, Virgin Gorda, Jost Van Dyke, and Anegada—plus 32 smaller islands of varying sizes.

Of the three U.S. Virgins, St. John is by far the most pristine of the group, thanks mainly to the creation in 1956 of the Virgin Islands National Park. The park started with 5,000 acres. Over the years it has grown steadily in size. Today it encompasses most of the island's land mass and includes many thousands of acres of offshore coral reefs.

As visitors approach St. John by boat, what they first see is a delightful panorama of rugged hills and uneven mountains. Next comes a chain of dazzling, palm-studded beaches. Once ashore, the exotic sights, sounds, and smells of this tropical paradise abound. Dotting the pictorial landscape are the now silent ruins of once prosperous plantations, stoic reminders of a colonial era when "sugar was king." Whether walking, hiking, sailing, horseback riding, or swimming, the history and beauty of the island are inescapable.

First and foremost, most visitors come to St. John to enjoy its natural surroundings. Of special note, naturally, are its gorgeous beaches. Their crystal-clear waters and sugar-white sands are without doubt some of the finest in the world. Further complementing these picture-perfect gems are clusters of spectacular reefs. The reefs are habitat to a kaleidoscopic array of multicolored fish and marine life waiting to delight swimmers and snorkelers of all ages.

Each year, an average of 500,000 tourists visit this tiny jewel, home to just 4,000 permanent residents. The principal port of entry and center of commerce is the small village of Cruz Bay. There are no airstrips on St. John, and no traffic lights. Although some visitors arrive by cruise ship, most make the final leg of their journey by ferrying over from neighboring St. Thomas. The nearest point of departure from St. Thomas to St. John is Red Hook (a 30-minute drive from the airport). Red Hook has regularly scheduled car and passenger ferry service. It takes less than 20 minutes to traverse the scenic passage. There is also a 45-minute public ferry (no cars) that runs between the towns of Charlotte Amalie (just 5 minutes from the airport) and Cruz Bay. This trip takes longer than a departure from Red Hook, but the views of the passing shoreline are well-worth the lengthier crossing.

Commercial activity in the village of Cruz Bay is low-key, but there are a number of eateries and cafes and ample opportunity for duty-free shopping. The village is a convenient place to schedule diving expeditions, sailing excursions, fishing charters, hikes, nature walks, and other fun activities.

Getting Around

Four-wheel drive vehicles (especially Jeeps) are a popular and convenient way to get around. Cars can be rented either on St. John or at locations on St. Thomas, including the airport. Taxis are readily available for hire. Colorful group taxis called "safari buses" can usually be found lined up and waiting for arriving passengers near

National Park Visitor Center

the entrance to the Cruz Bay public dock. There is also public bus service (Vitran) that runs from Cruz Bay to Coral Bay and out to popular Salt Pond Beach on the south side of the island. Call Vitran for a schedule: (340) 774-0165. The Vitran bus route does not include stops at any of the north shore beaches such as Trunk Bay, Hawksnest, or Cinnamon Bay. Rental cars and taxis are the best way to reach these north shore destinations.

If you need internet services, fax machines, or telephones, visit Connections, the island communication center located on Prinsden Gade (Danish for "Prince Street") in the pink building across the park from the ferry dock. The National Park Visitor Center is also located in Cruz Bay *(see town map, p.40)*. Here you can obtain information about park programs, activities, and also purchase books and literature about the island.

If you happen to find yourself with extra time and have a hankering for a quick, island-hopping adventure, consider a day trip to the nearby British Virgin Islands. Ferry transportation to the BVI departs daily from the customs house in Cruz Bay.

About Our Guidebook

Our guidebook features three self-guided walking and motor tours designed to provide visitors with a meaningful introduction to the history and natural beauty of St. John. This is the third edition of our travel guide, which was first published in 1974. The current edition contains new photographs, images, and updated information about this beautiful island.

The guidebook begins with a brief history followed by a short narrative detailing the story of the creation of the Virgin Islands National Park. Next come three self-guided tours: *Walking Tour of Cruz Bay, North Shore Motor Tour,* and *Centerline Motor Tour to East End and South Shore.* Additionally, there are descriptive lists of popular beaches and hiking trails, including the three park service self-guided hikes: *Reef Bay Trail, Annaberg Ruins,* and *Cinnamon Bay Ruins & Loop Trail.* The park service has installed identification plaques along each of these trails, and much of the information from these plaques is included in our guidebook. At the back of the book, as a further resource, we have also included checklists of St. John's more common flora and fauna.

There is no set order to taking any of the hikes or tours. Some bring you to beaches offering an opportunity to combine sightseeing with a picnic and swim.

Local Customs and Useful Tips

- Remember to drive on the left. Wear seat belts. Children must use car seats if they are five years old or younger or weigh less than 40 pounds. Fines can be stiff!
- Islanders are in the habit of greeting each other with a friendly "Good Morning" or "Good Afternoon" before commencing conversation. Try it! It's a nice custom to observe.
- The sun shines very intensely here. When at the beach, wear sun block, and lots of it! We recommend a liberal application of a reef-safe product and perhaps a cap or wide-brimmed hat. The V.I. Legislature has banned sunscreens known to cause harm to the reefs and marine life.
- When hiking in forests and damp environments, mosquito repellent is recommended. Efforts are made to control the island mosquito population, but mosquito-borne strains of the zika virus, dengue fever, and other insect-related illnesses do occasionally appear on St. John.
- Please safeguard your valuables. Try to keep them with you at all times. When away from your lodging, if you leave valuables behind, lock your doors or place them in your hotel safe. Do not leave them in unlocked vehicles.
- Most island residents are very modest people. Women are expected not to wear bathing suits in town, and men should always cover-up their chests and wear shirts.

For your personal safety and welfare, remember to exercise the same cautions you would back home. When visiting remote beaches, hiking trails, and less populated areas, it's always best to play it safe and go with others in a group. When walking the streets of downtown Cruz Bay after dark, it's a good precaution to stick to main roads and well-lighted areas.

History

Early Visitors, Inhabitants, and Colonization

The first inhabitants of the Virgin Islands probably date back to around 1500 B.C. when now extinct Ciboney people lived in the area. Remnants of their Stone Age tools have been found, but little more. The Ciboneys were followed by Arawaks, who began showing up around 300 A.D. Arawaks were an agrarian people who sustained themselves by growing cotton, tobacco, yucca, guava, and other crops. Arawaks were eventually assimilated into the broader Taino culture (Taino/Arawaks), which proliferated throughout the region up until the early 1550s, when their numbers began to decline with the arrival of Spanish conquerors who enslaved and subjected them to hard labor from which many perished. Contact

Carib Family, John Stedman, 1818, Courtesy Wikipedia, PD-1923, https://commons.wikimedia.org/wiki/File:Carib_indian_family_by_John_Gabriel_Stedman.jpg

with western Europeans also resulted in deadly diseases against which the indigenous population had no immunity.

Taino/Arawaks were living on St. John up until the fifteenth century. They were ultimately extinguished by waves of warlike Caribs, who began arriving in the area from Guiana. In 1493 Columbus encountered hostile Caribs while on his second voyage to the New World. The hostilities are believed to have taken place on nearby St. Croix, or possibly St. Martin. Wanting to avoid any further trouble with Caribs, Columbus did not go ashore upon reaching St. John. However, the beauty and large grouping of the islands apparently reminded him of the fabled tale of Saint Ursula and her army of virgins who were massacred by the Huns for refusing to marry them, so Columbus named the cluster *"Santa Úrsula y Las Once Mil Vírgnes (St. Ursula and the Eleven Thousand Virgins),"* before sailing on.

Columbus was the first European explorer to create lasting interest in the New World. His sponsoring country, Spain, was quick to see the profit potential of his discoveries, which became the centerpiece of Spain's early colonization efforts in the Americas. At the beginning of the 1600s, Spain was the dominant European force in the eastern Caribbean. But that did not last long. Other European countries quickly saw the potential of the region and started challenging Spain's monopoly.

It was on his second voyage that Columbus became the first European to bring sugar cane from its native habitat in Asia to the Caribbean. It was planted in the Dominican Republic and observed to thrive well in the tropical climate. Sugar was already a highly prized commodity in western Europe, and other countries besides Spain were eager to take advantage of the benefits of sugar-cane cultivation in the Caribbean. The West Indies were a much closer and safer distance to travel than was the long voyage to Asia. Soon settlers from England, France, Denmark, and Holland were looking for opportunities to establish colonies. This resulted in a series of clashes as competing nations jockeyed amongst themselves and Spain for control of Caribbean islands.

Although early records are sketchy, it is reasonable to assume that St. John's first European inhabitants were probably Dutch

HISTORY 19

settlers, migrating from nearby Tortola and Virgin Gorda in the late 1600s. The growing Dutch presence on Tortola and Virgin Gorda was an on-going problem for Spanish authorities. Spanish soldiers made several unsuccessful attempts at dislodging them by dispatching troops from Puerto Rico. However, each time, as soon as the Spanish military departed, determined Dutch "squatters" would return and rebuild their settlements.

Towards the end of the seventeenth century, England also began showing an interest in Tortola and Virgin Gorda. Colonies were established, seemingly with no meaningful opposition from the home governments of either Holland or Spain. However, the presence of the English settlers did lead to friction with the Dutch inhabitants, and there were on-going skirmishes. The hostilities were finally put to rest in 1672, when a seasoned detachment of British troops arrived and succeeded in permanently overrunning the poorly protected Dutch settlements. Their elimination enabled England to formally claim Tortola and Virgin Gorda as Crown colonies.

Some of the Dutch settlers displaced by these altercations managed to relocate to nearby St. Thomas, which Denmark was at the time in the process of colonizing. A few likely settled secretly on St. John, as well.

The Danish presence in the Virgin Islands officially began in 1671 with the granting of a Danish royal charter to the West India and Guinea Company. This broadly written document gave the Company the governing rights over St. Thomas and the "surrounding islands," which Danish officials interpreted to include St. John. The Company was all powerful. It had control over determining how plantations were divided-up and awarded, and it had a monopoly on all trade with the Danish West Indies. It maintained this authority up until 1754 when the Danish Crown finally dissolved the Company and assumed administrative control of its islands.

The presence of the English on Tortola and the Danes on nearby St. Thomas caught St. John in a tug of war. From the start, there were problems. Both sides felt they had a claim to tiny St. John. At first there were a few brave souls (some Danish; others perhaps Dutch) who openly made unsanctioned attempts at setting up homesteads on the island. Each time, the would-be inhabitants were harassed and driven away by British authorities. Eventually Denmark decided to assume a more assertive stance. In March 1718, a formal "takeover" was staged with a landing in Coral Bay led by Governor Bredal. The event was glowingly described as follows in the governor's report to Company directors:

> *There I have planted the flag of our most gracious king, and fired a Danish salute and we have eaten, and drunk the health of our most gracious king and then of the success of the Honorable Company. Since then I have chosen a place to build a fort that is quite comfortable and commands the entrance of the harbor itself and, in addition to that, a plain below on which a village can be founded .... I asked the planters to estimate the soil there, which they praised, and I have selected a field for the plantation of the Honorable Company at a distance of gunshot from where the fort is to be built. - ("The Danish Colonization of St. John 1718-1733," by* **Lief Calundann Larsen, pp. 20-21.)**

The English were naturally upset by Bredal's actions. Dire consequences were threatened, but nothing came of the matter. Despite the saber-rattling, the formal occupation progressed, and eventually St. John fell firmly under Danish control.

The Danish takeover of St. John was largely about expanding its sugar interests. Soil conditions on St. Thomas were starting to deteriorate, and there was the belief that more fertile soil could be found on St. John. To encourage planters to extend their sugar cultivation from St. Thomas to St. John, the government granted St. Thomas planters the privilege of being absentee owners by allowing them to hire overseers to manage their St. John properties. They were also given the right to take, without charge, as much wood and lime as they needed to build their sugar works. As a final inducement, planters were granted a seven-year tax abatement. The incentives worked, and plantations were soon being established at a number of locations.

In a 1726 account to Company directors, Governor Frederick Moth sent the following glowing report:

HISTORY

St. Jan is now so populated that no lots are left, except in the vicinity of the fortress and the Company plantation. ...Next year the inhabitants of St. Jan will begin to pay personal and land taxes. There are nearly 20 sugar works, some already built and some under construction, so I think that next year St. Jan will yield more than 600,000 to 800,000 pounds of sugar in addition to cotton-on all of which taxes must be paid.- (**"The Danish Coloniza-tion of St. John 1718-1733," by Leif Calundann Larsen, pp. 30-31 combined with a portion of Larsen's earlier translation of the governor's letter as it appeared in "St. John Voices," by Ruth Hull Low, p.1.)**

At first, government officials imagined that early profits from St. John's sugar plantations would continue to grow indefinitely. This false sense of confidence went on for a decade or more. Then planters started complaining that soil conditions were not quite as good as what had originally been assumed. The initial euphoria was further deflated by Denmark's purchase of the much larger island of St. Croix, coming just fifteen years after settlement of St. John. St. Croix's larger size and flatter landscape were, by comparison, viewed as more conducive to large-scale sugar cultivation. This realization led to a reluctance to make further investments in sugar production on St. John, and less profitable crops such as cotton and tobacco were gradually introduced.

Enslaved Labor Trade

As a general rule, profit margins from a successful sugar works were thin, and expenses had to be carefully calculated and monitored. Having an available, cost-effective labor supply was a critical component for success. There were early experiments with the use of convicts as forced labor, but convicts were not a large enough source to meet the fast growing demand for plantation labor, and planters early on became more and more reliant on the ready availability of enslaved labor. By the time the Danish settlement on St. John had taken root, Danish trans-Atlantic trafficking of enslaved African labor was well underway.

The Danes officially entered the enslaved labor trade in 1657 by building a fort, "Fort Christianborg," near Accra on the west coast of Guinea in what was known as the Amina district. The Akwamu were the dominant tribe in the area. At first the Danes obtained enslaved laborers from the Akwamu, who waged war on other tribes and delivered their captives to the Danes. However, after a powerful Akwamu king died, rival tribes became emboldened and began attacking the Akwamu. In 1730, the Akwamu suffered a decisive defeat and lost control of the area. In retaliation for years of Akwamu oppression, the victorious tribes began selling Akwamu captives to the Danes. Some ended up on St. John. These proud Akwamu warriors now found themselves forced to work side-by-side with some of their former captives, causing discord. Inter-tribal enmities were to play a key role in the historic Revolt of 1733.

Human trafficking was being practiced at the time by all European powers with plantation interests in the West Indies. It was an integral part of the "Triangular Trade," a multi-faceted barter system that crisscrossed the Atlantic.

The three-legged triangle depended on the following: European merchants shipping goods to the west coast of Africa where the cargo was exchanged for captured inhabitants; enslaved Africans transported to the West Indies or American colonies, where they

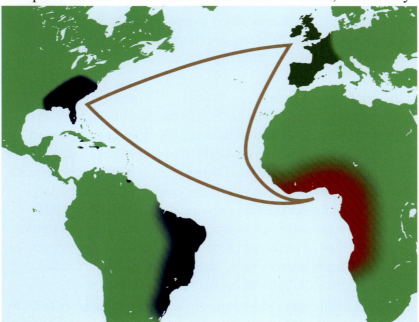

Sémhur, Triangular Trade, Courtesy Wikimedia under creative commons license, https://commons.wikimedia.org/wiki/File:Triangular_trade.svg

HISTORY

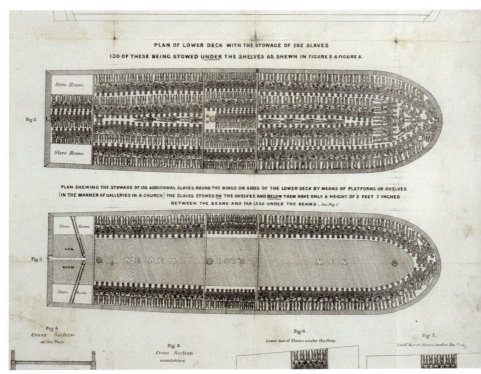

Cargo Plan for Enslaved Laborers on Ship "Brooks," Courtesy Wikipedia, PD, https://commons. wikimedia.org/wiki/File:Slaveshipposter.jpg

were sold or traded for cotton, sugar, rum, tobacco, and other goods; and cargo that was then carried back to Europe and again sold or exchanged for goods bound for Africa.

Danish trading companies followed two routes to the Danish West Indies: the *triangular route* (picking up captives) and the more commonly used *direct route* (trading for goods only). By the middle of the eighteenth century, 96% of ships leaving Denmark for the West Indies followed the direct route; only 4% actually made the stop in Guinea to pick-up enslaved laborers. During the height of the human trafficking years, Denmark became the seventh largest trafficker of enslaved laborers. Records indicate that one hundred and twenty thousand enslaved persons were carried to the West Indies under the Danish flag. Other countries added significantly to this abusive practice. Collectively, European nations transported over a million enslaved persons across the Atlantic to the West Indies and America between 1500 and 1800.

The three-legged Atlantic passage took two to three months to complete. Living conditions aboard the enslaved labor ships were abominable. In the cargo plan *(previous page)* for the transport ship *Brookes*, each adult man was allotted a space measuring only 71 inches by 16 inches with just 31.5 inches up to the next layer of captives. The *Brooks* plan could accommodate 450 enslaved laborers. Captives were forced to lie without relief in their extremely cramped spaces for months. Many died from disease; some deliberately starved themselves to death. Fatalities varied widely from one passage to another. Documents in the Danish National Archives reveal that during the period 1777-1789 an estimated average of 16% of the captives died on each crossing. The highest mortality rate of 45% for ships completing the passage was reported for the ship *Accra* in 1781. However, sometimes ships never completed the journey, and everyone perished. The Danes officially ended their enslaved labor trade in 1803.

Life as an Enslaved Laborer

Once here, enslaved Africans were further subjected to deplorable and inhumane living conditions. It is difficult for us today to comprehend how people, not so long ago, could so readily have employed the wide-spread practice of enslavement. Unfortunately, even as recently as the early 1700s, it was not the common belief that all people were born with the same basic human rights that most of us now take for granted. Back then, if you were unlucky enough to enter this world at the bottom of the social-economic ladder, you were pretty much destined for a life of arduous work, hardship, and toil.

During the Danish colonial period, when an enslaved laborer was sold to a plantation owner, that unfortunate soul became the official "property" of the owner. The owner could do as he wished with his purchase. Owners often raped female captives as a matter of right. They were free to punish enslaved laborers as they saw fit. Owners also had the right to sell children and could send them away from their parents. Basic rules were eventually drawn-up as to how enslaved persons were to be treated, but observance of these "rules" was highly discretionary and contradictory.

Revolt of 1733

St. John's planters and others in the ruling class lived in constant fear of insurrection. But it was a series of extreme back-to-back events that heightened tensions and made 1733 especially difficult. The year began with a severe drought during the spring and summer months that caused damage to the enslaved inhabitants' maize, sweet potato, and other subsistence crops. This brought on hunger and fears of starvation, which resulted in unrest and thieving. The drought was followed by a ferocious hurricane in July of that year, which brought further damage to crops and caused more uneasiness. Next came a plague of insects, followed by another fierce storm. The already tense situation was further aggravated by a number of harsh laws issued by Governor Gardelin in early September. The new laws were aimed at tempering disobedience, however, they had the opposite effect. Lashings, brandings, and loss of limbs were legalized as punishment for any captive thought to be plotting or acting disrespectfully towards a plantation owner. If an enslaved person committed a theft or tried to run away and was caught, he could be pinched with red-hot tongs, have a limb cut off, or be hanged.

By the end of October tempers had reached a boiling point, and things were beginning to deteriorate fast. Enslaved laborers from several plantations had begun to "go maroon" (run away) and hide in the bush.

It's the common belief that the primary instigators of the rebellion were a group of captives from the once dominant Akwamu tribe who had recently arrived together at the Suhm Plantation in Coral Bay. These were once high-ranking Akwamu warriors who could not easily adjust themselves to enslavement. So the leaders of the group at Suhm began carefully plotting a revolt. The rebels were so confident of winning that they even planned an early division of spoils and cautioned against destroying buildings they thought could be used by them after they took control of the island and established their own nation.

The trigger point came early Monday morning, November 23rd, around 2:00 a.m., when several Akwamu staged a surprise attack on the guards at Fort Frederiksvaern in Coral Bay. Six guards were killed. One guard, Jan Gabriel, escaped by hiding under a bed. He then made his way over to St. Thomas where he alerted officials. In the meantime, the rebels fired a cannon at the fort to signal the start of the revolt. Others joined in, and by morning the rebel group had grown to about eighty in number. Initially, the rebels split into two groups. One moved along the north shore threatening planters and forcing them to take refuge at the Duurloo Plantation (Caneel Bay). The second group stayed at the main encampment at the Suhm Plantation and kept watch on the fort.

At the Carolina Estate in Coral Bay, John Sodtmann, a planter and local judge, and his young stepdaughter were among the first to perish. Fortunately, Sodtmann's wife was on St. Thomas at the time. However, many other planters and family members succumbed to the rebels in the early hours of the revolt.

After word of the insurrection reached St. Thomas, the Danes sent aid. A support force was dispatched and arrived at Duurloo late in the day on November 23rd to reinforce the planters and workers who had taken refuge there. A second group of soldiers arrived at Coral Bay on November 25th. They reclaimed the fort and overcame the rebels at the Suhm Plantation, forcing them to scatter into the woods. But the rebels were not discouraged and kept up the fight. The English on Tortola and St. Kitts followed with similar attempts at crushing the revolt, but they were also unsuccessful. Reports to the Company directors began to suggest that the Danes were in for a long and difficult struggle. As the months went by, the Danes became more and more dejected with their futile efforts to subdue the revolt. Finally, Danish authorities called upon the French for assistance. The French eagerly offered help as they were at the time anxious to win Danish support for French policies in the Baltic.

In April 1734, French authorities dispatched a full company of 200 soldiers, who arrived on St. John in two warships. This led to order being restored, but only after seven long months of successful resistance by a much smaller, courageous group of rebel fighters. The following is a series of excerpts detailing the suppression taken from an account of events by Monsieur le Chevalier de Longueville, commander of the French expeditionary force, upon his return to the port of Guadeloupe:

I arrived on that island [St. Thomas] on Wednesday the 23rd of April after a nine-day crossing. I set sail the following day at dawn and came to anchor at 2:00 in the afternoon in the harbor of St. John [Coral Bay], which is only seven leagues from St. Thomas. I immediately disembarked everyone and then put them to work with all diligence stretching the sails which had been given to us in St. Thomas to serve as tents, I then drew up details to insure the security of the camp. That night the rain fell so heavily that we were nearly flooded. It lasted almost 30 hours at the same intensity; at that point there were scarcely ten weapons capable of being fired. Everyone remained up; I withdrew the sentries who had become useless and unable to fight.

On Tuesday the 28th of April, I ordered the arms distributed in order to organize detachments to enter the woods....While coming down a ravine..., my advanced guard spotted 12 or 13 of the rebels whose indiscreet gunshot fired on Nadau's detachment....One of them was killed and one of my men was slightly wounded in the arm by a number three gunshot fired by those wretches. While pursuing them, I found the spot where they lived in the middle of the ravine at the bottom of a precipice. There were 26 huts both large and small. I had the huts set on fire and continued to give chase until dark.... The next three days proved fruitless though they were nonetheless tiresome. The continual rain during the 32 days I spent on the island contributed in no small way to increased fatigue.

On Sunday, May 2nd, I returned to camp....In the evening, a resident of St. Thomas on his way to Spanishtown, an English island [Virgin Gorda], came to warn me that he had seen smoke on a point [probably Ram Head] and that it had to be the rebels since they were the ones in the woods....Right away, I ordered the formation of two detachments of 45 men under the command of Messieurs Nadau and Lignery who ...left the next day two hours before daybreak, expecting to reach the indicated spot under cover of night, since the resident of St. Thomas had assured me that it was only an hour away; however, it took three hours with the result the rebels espied from a good distance the movement of the detachments and fled, burning their huts behind them. We found one whom they had killed the day before and one who hanged himself as my men approached.... Since that time, we neither saw nor encountered the rebels.... The rebels had retired to the point with the plan of killing themselves.... In order to learn the truth of the matter, I sent an officer with a detachment to that place.... They found only eleven bodies among which were those of two women.

On Sunday the 23rd, [we] discovered... the spot where the rebels met with their final defeat. There were 25 of them in all with six women among their number....

Seeing that...all these miserable wretches had destroyed themselves and that there remained nothing more to do, I prepared for our departure.... – **(Excerpt from a document published in *The French Intervention in the St. John Slave Revolt of 1733-34,* translated by Aimery P. Caron and Arnold R Highfield, pp. 41-44.)**

The rebellion on St. John was historic because it was one of the earliest, most organized, and most successful enslaved labor revolts in the history of man's struggle for freedom and equality. The plan was to take the planters and soldiers by surprise. Things went well at first, but then bogged down. The biggest problem faced by the rebels was the fact that they did not have enough guns and ammunition. The second problem was that not everyone joined the revolt, which may have had something to do with inter-tribal hostilities. Had more participated in the struggle, things could very well have gone differently. It took another hundred years before another successful revolt could be organized and freedom achieved.

The monetary and personal cost of the revolt was considered huge at the time, estimated at 7,905 rigsdalers. About a quarter of the white population was killed. Of the 1,414 enslaved workers on the island, about 90 were believed to have been fully involved in the revolt. Most of the rebels were killed in the conflict; 27 were tried and executed. The effects of the revolt were long-lasting and many planters fled to St. Croix, never to return.

Transition from Colonization

Although sugar production continued to be marginally profitable for many years after the rebellion, there were a variety of factors, besides the revolt itself, that were major contributors to the ultimate decline of the island's sugar-based economy. One was the havoc caused by the Napoleonic Wars (1790-1815), which found

Denmark aligned with France against England. This gave British troops on Tortola the perfect excuse to invade St. John. They twice attacked and occupied the island, once briefly in 1801 and again in 1807. The second occupation lasted seven years and had a damaging impact on the island's economy.

The introduction of the European sugar beet in the early 1800s was a big factor, as well. Sugar beets could be cultivated and harvested cheaply and did not require a warm tropical climate. This enhanced the volume and profitability of sugar-beet crop production.

Carolina Estate, One Hundred Years After the Revolt, Frederik von Scholten, 1833, Courtesy Maritime Museum of Denmark, PD, https://commons.wikimedia.org/wiki/File:Frederik_von_Scholten_-_Carolina_at_Coral_Bay,_St._Jan.jpg

There were also topographic issues with St. John's limited land mass and mountainous terrain, which made large-scale sugar production more difficult and costly than elsewhere.

St. John planters worked hard to try and stay competitive by experimenting with various expense-cutting methods, the more notable being the introduction of new and hardier strains of sugar cane and the use of steam-powered equipment, both of which offered some relief.

The economic impact of abolition further compounded the financial burdens of planters. Formal Emancipation in the Danish islands came about when thousands of enslaved laborers gathered on St. Croix on July 2, 1848, threatening to burn down the town of Frederiksted if they were not granted freedom. Governor Peter von Scholten acquiesced to the demand. On July 3-4, a poster was printed and published throughout the Danish islands *(see p. 30)*. The English version of the bilingual text read as follows:

1. All Unfree in the Danish West India Islands are from to-day Emancipated. 2. The ...[freed laborers] retain for three months from date the use of the houses and provision grounds of which they have hither-to been possessed. 3. Labour is in future to be paid for by agreement, but allowance is to cease. 4. The maintenance of old and infirmed, who are not able to work is until further determination to be furnished by the late owners.

Emancipation Poster, Courtesy Wikimedia under creative commons license, PD, https://commons.wikimedia.org/wiki/File:EmancipationsplakatDWI1848.jpg

It was the collective sequence of these cited events that hobbled and eventually crumbled the economy, causing St. John's struggling sugar plantations, one-by-one, to cease operations. The last to shut down was Reef Bay in 1916.

The collapsed sugar economy was replaced by an era of subsistence farming and cottage industry. Efforts were made by the Danish government to revive the deflated economy by persuading planters and nobility to purchase and cultivate land. Books were written about the abundance of agricultural crops that could be grown here. At the turn of the century, experimental cultivation stations were set up on St. Thomas and St. Croix to enhance agricultural production. Attempts were made to encourage various industries such as honey and egg production, as well as harvesting of salt and the manufacturing of bay oil. However, these efforts (while noteworthy) failed to bring about significant improvement to the economy.

At the turn of the century, Danish journalist Olaf Linck, while on a visit with Count Henrik and his new bride Countess Daisy, paints an unpromising picture of the status of St. John's land use and the prospect for any future enhancement of its productivity:

HISTORY

It is almost sunset when we reach our destination, the mountain Bordeaux, with the plantation "Lamesure," which is owned by ... [Count Henrik]. Practically the whole island of St Jan is over-grown with bush, where only a few generations ago there were sugar and cotton fields.

[Count Henrik] is one of the few in our time who has bought land on St. Jan in order to cultivate it.... On the entire island only about three or four plantations are under cultivation; one of these is America Hill, owned by a Danish company which is going in for cattle breeding. For some years there have been experiments with crossing native cattle with Danish and English cattle, and it seems to work out well. So, there should be a future for cattle breeding on St. Jan....

On Saturday all work on the land stops, and most men fit for work will sail out for fishing. Mostly they come back with their boats full of fish in all colors of the rainbow. When these fish are salted, there is food in the hut for most of the week.

Governor Helwig-Larsen has long been aware of the possi-bilities....[He] tried to get the Danish nobility and gentleman farmers interested, while reasoning that it would be a worthwhile task for these men to buy land on St. Jan and cultivate it. So, he invited them to a meeting where it might be discussed, but those he had counted on most did not attend. So, the matter was shelved.... It has also been suggested that uncultivated land be taxed and a tax rebate be given to cultivated land.... The Co-lonial Council, at least, doesn't feel the time is right for such experiments. – **(St. John Backtime, by Ruth Hull Low & Rafael Valls, pp. 50-51.)**

Purchase of the Virgin Islands by the United States was the outcome of more than a half century of negotiations with Den-mark. After a number of false starts an agreement was concluded, and the formal change of flags took place on March 31, 1917. The purchase price was $25 million (a large sum at the time). There is speculation that the U.S. decision to acquire the Virgin Islands may have been influenced mostly by growing fears that the German government might end up purchasing them and use the harbors as bases for U-boat attacks. The sale of the Virgin Islands was not met with unanimous approval by the Danish populous. Even today, many Danes look back on the loss of their West Indian possessions with regret.

Of the three major islands in the group, St. John seemed at the time of transfer the least promising to most observers. A U.S. Department of Commerce report, published in 1916, offers the following assessment of the island:

> *St. John may be left entirely out of consideration so far as the market for boots and shoes is concerned. It is smaller than either St. Thomas or St. Croix, with a population of some 800... natives. Conditions are everywhere extremely primitive, and it is safe to say that not more than 8% of the inhabitants have ever worn a pair of shoes in their lives. There are no stores of any description, all purchases being made on the neighboring island of St. Thomas.* - **(Excerpt from U.S. Department of Commerce Reports, 1916 in anticipation of transfer. Courtesy of** *St. John Voices,* **"Observations of the Island," by Ruth Hull Low, p. 5.)**

There were a few positive reports expounding on St. John's economic potential, but little was done during the first two decades of U.S. ownership to take advantage of opportunities to enhance the general welfare of the population. St. John's primary industries of bay oil production, charcoal manufacturing, basketmaking, and animal husbandry produced pockets of economic success, but, overall living conditions remained extremely primitive.

However, following the end of WWII things changed. Tourism suddenly blossomed throughout the Caribbean. Visitors began arriving in droves, and the economy suddenly improved. The big trigger points accelerating the tourist boom on St. John were the development of the Caneel Bay Resort and the creation of the Virgin Islands National Park.

Creation of the Virgin Islands National Park

The Virgin Islands National Park was made possible in large part through the help and generosity of Laurance S. Rockefeller (1910-2004). Rockefeller's love of nature sprung from his many childhood vacations at national parks with his family. In 1991, President George W. Bush awarded him the Congressional Gold Medal for his tireless efforts in the field of conservation.

Rockefeller first set eyes on St. John while on a sailing vacation with his wife in 1952. The couple dropped anchor at Caneel Bay, where they discovered a small hotel. Rockefeller eventually purchased the property and developed the hotel into a world-renowned luxury resort. From the moment he first stepped ashore, Rockefeller began to appreciate the need to safeguard and preserve the unique and fragile beauty of the island. Other visionaries at the time included Frank Stick, an American artist, who had come to St. John to draw illustrations of fish. Shortly after arriving, Stick and four partners purchased 1,433 acres of land on the south side of the island. Their holdings included Lameshur Estate and Reef Bay. At first the group planned to use the land for development. However, Stick quickly abandoned those plans and instead began a quest to use the property for the creation of a park. To promote the idea, Stick wrote a letter to the then Virgin Islands' governor, Archie Alexander, outlining his plan. He included in his letter a copy of a 1939 proposal by Harold Hubler, another forward thinker who also wanted to see a national park created on St. John. The governor was favorably moved by Stick's overture and vowed to support the effort. Hearing of Rockefeller's similar interest in preserving St. John, Stick copied Rockefeller on his letter. Shortly thereafter, the two reached an agreement to pursue their common goal together.

Laurance Rockefeller Philanthropist

In 1956 Laurance S. Rockefeller, financier and conservationist, donated over 5,000 acres through the Jackson Hole Preserve for the establishment of Virgin Islands National Park. While sailing the Caribbean in 1952, he became enchanted with the people and the unspoiled beauty of St. John. The unique natural, cultural and historic resources of the park are protected in perpetuity, thanks to his vision and generosity.

Rockefeller at Caneel Bay, Courtesy of the NPS, PD

Stick, acting as the front man quietly arranged options for the acquisition of much of the original 5,000 acres of what was to become the future park. In some cases, Stick used personal funds to help pay for the necessary options. He also contributed his own land to the venture. Once secured, the rights to the original 5,000 acres were then transferred to the Rockefeller-controlled Jackson

STJ ON FOOT AND BY CAR

Hole Preserve. They were later purchased and donated by Rockefeller to the federal government for the creation of the park. The bill authorizing the establishment of the Virgin Islands National Park was signed by President Eisenhower on August 2, 1956. On the day that the deeds were transferred to the U.S. government, a celebration took place that lived long in the memory of many St. John residents. Rockefeller hosted a dinner party at Caneel Bay, and the entire island was invited:

> *The entire island population including the aged and infirmed and tiny babies...[was] seven hundred and twenty. They all came to dinner. Some traveled by donkey and some by boat. There were dignitaries from New York and some two hundred visitors from other islands. The New York Herald Tribune carried a story headlined "Nine Hundred and Twenty Get Barbecued Pig in Virgin Islands."*
>
> *Andromeda Keating and her twin sister Myrah, headed-up a battalion of women who ladled out the food as the long line marched past with plates in hand. The Keatings had cooked some five hundred pounds of meat in their outside ovens for the party. In addition, hams were baked and turkeys roasted by the chef at Caneel Bay Plantation. The two hundred pounds of pig was charcoal broiled in St. Thomas and came over on the "Chocolate Queen." Hundreds of cans of free beer were consumed. And, of course, barrels and barrels of the favorite drink of the islands, rum punch. After the speeches, the flag-raising, and playing of the Star-Spangled Banner, calypso bands took over and everybody danced.* – **(George T. Eggleston,** *Virgin Islands* **pp. 141-144. Reproduced with special permission of Krieger Publishing and Eggleston family members.) Eggleston was a cartoonist, yachtsman, author, editor, and a leading U.S. spokesman on political issues leading up to and after the bombing of Pearl Harbor during World War II.**

Today the park includes most of the north shore and much of the central and southeast portions of the island, including 7,259 acres of terrestrial and shoreline habitat and 5,650 acres of adjacent submerged land (offshore underwater habitat, added to the park in 1962). The park also includes 128 acres on Hassel Island in Charlotte Amalie Harbor on St. Thomas, which was added in 1978. In 2001, the Virgin Islands Coral Reef National Monument was es-

HISTORY

tablished to protect 12,708 acres of submerged land and associated marine resources around the island. In summary, the park service manages almost 58% of the land area of St. John and more than 18,000 acres of offshore underwater habitat.

The park offers protection to coral reefs, seagrass beds, mangroves, and other marine habitats that support sea turtles, corals, and marine life. It also protects some of the last remaining native tropical dry rain forest in the Caribbean. In 1976 the Virgin Islands National Park was designated an International Biosphere Reserve by the United Nations Educational, Scientific, and Cultural Organization (UNESCO). Of the hundreds of UNESCO biosphere reserves worldwide, this park is 1 of 30 reserves containing both marine and terrestrial ecosystems. It provides a vital habitat for over 144 bird species, 400 reef-associated fish species, 17 species of whales and dolphins, 13 reptile species, numerous sponges, and more than 45 stony coral species. Several marine and terrestrial species are federally listed as endangered or threatened. The park's cultural resources are abundant and diverse, including prehistoric archeological sites, hundreds of historic structures, offshore shipwrecks, and museum collections that encompass artifacts dating as far back as 840 B.C. when Ciboney and later Taino/Arawak and Carib people lived in the area. Ruins of more than 100 plantations that existed on the island during the sugar production years are located within park boundaries. Some are stabilized and maintained. Three of these—Reef Bay, Annaberg, and Cinnamon Bay—are heavily visited. The park uses them

Boundary Map, Courtesy NPS, PD

STJ ON FOOT AND BY CAR

to interpret the European economic expansion and associated enslavement of Africans. Ranger-guided hikes provide a history of sugar production in the Reef Bay Valley.

The park suffered extensive underwater and terrestrial damage from the 2017 monster hurricanes, Irma and Maria. However, thanks to the incredible efforts and coordination of park trail crews, the Army Corps of Engineers, the disaster relief team, Friends of the National Park, and other volunteers, the park is on a steady path to recovery and all trails and beaches are again open to the public.

This park belongs to all people, and the park service asks that all visitors do their part to help preserve this wonderful natural resource for the welfare of everyone by adhering to park rules and regulations. The following activities are prohibited within park boundaries:

- Drug and alcohol use
- Pets off-leash
- Camping outside of designated campgrounds
- Fires outside of park-provided fire rings or grills
- Littering or dumping
- Loud parties in campgrounds
- Other illegal activities or safety problems

DRONES ARE NOT ALLOWED IN THE NATIONAL PARK FOR ANY PURPOSE.

TO REPORT POSSIBLE VIOLATIONS, CALL PARK WATCH AT 1-866-995-8467.

Walking Tour of Cruz Bay
(2.5 Hours, Approx.)

Cruz Bay, nicknamed "Love City," is the busy village setting that is the heartbeat of the island. Here you'll find numerous shops and restaurants. The National Park Visitor Center, post office, police station, and government offices are also located in Cruz Bay. The town (originally founded as "Christiansbay") dates to the earliest colonial days and was placed on the National Register of Historic Places in 2016. Cruz Bay totals approximately 15 acres on which there are approximately 25 buildings of contributing historical significance. These structures reflect the two distinct influences of the town's Danish (pretransfer) and North American pasts. Examples of these two influences are noted on the walking tour. *(For a detailed description of these historic buildings and their architectural and cultural significance, readers may want to visit/download the Cruz Bay Town, Historic Places Registration Form at https:// www.nps.gov/nr/feature/places/pdfs/16000699.pdf. Another useful reference is "An Historical Walking Map of Cruz Bay," published by the St. John Historical Society. The map can be purchased online for $10 on the Historical Society website at https://stjohn-historicalsociety.org.)*

Our tour starts at the visitor center. Included on the route are the Lind Point Overlook, popular Honeymoon Beach, Friend's store at Mongoose Junction, Administration "Battery" Building, Francis Powell Park, historic cemeteries, Frank Bay Beach, and the Elaine Sprauve Library. Along the way you'll learn about local customs and foods and will be introduced to notable personalities.

Brief History of the Town

The first official recognition of Cruz Bay as a town came in the year 1766, when Julius von Rohr was commissioned by the Danish Crown to create a survey of the settlement. Von Rohr's map shows a simple village. The only existing structures were three military facilities (consisting of a barracks, kitchen, and officers' quarters)

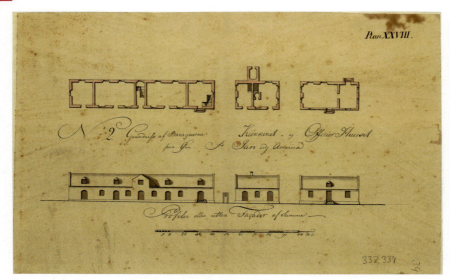

Peter Oxholm Drawing of Cruz Bay Military Buildings, 1780, PD, Courtesy of the Danish National Archives, https://www.virgin-islands-history.org/en/history/ownership-history/oxholms-west-indies-maps-and-drawings-st-john/

along with three private homes, which were likely reserved for visiting officials. Despite its small size, the natural harbor of Cruz Bay was a convenient shipping point for those St. John planters who did not own seaside property.

It was not until the end of the eighteenth century, when skilled tradesmen and service providers began arriving, that the town started to grow. The new inhabitants were mostly former enslaved persons turned tradesmen. Freed tradesmen residing in town typically used their Cruz Bay homes as their living quarters and places of business. Their various services included sewing, boat building, fishing, carpentry, and masonry work.

Unfortunately, in many ways these freed persons were not so "free." Chances for freed persons to improve their economic mobility and social status were extremely limited. While there was a law granting them a "cer-

Jack Delano, Cruz Bay Dock, 1941, Courtesy of Library of Congress, https://www.loc.gov/item/2017797801/

WALKING TOUR OF CRUZ BAY

tificate of freedom," there were conflicting regulations that restricted their social standing and hindered opportunity for economic improvement. One law denied them the right to obtain business licenses, which white inhabitants were readily being granted. In 1834, a Royal Ordinance was finally passed granting freed persons equal status with whites.

Despite social and economic obstacles, the Cruz Bay population grew steadily, and by 1831 there was a recorded census reading of 100 intown inhabitants.

The collapse of the sugar economy in the late 1800s reversed the trend. People gradually started departing the town. By the end of the century, only a few hardy souls remained. Not even the transfer of ownership to the United States in 1917 brought much improvement. But the boom in tourism following WWII was a game-changer. Economic prosperity returned, and the new influx of tourists quickly transformed Cruz Bay into the busy harbor community you see today.

Start of Walking Tour

The walking tour begins at the National Park Visitor Center. The center offers exhibits, brochures, maps, and educational books regarding the natural and cultural history of the park. Park rangers can tell you about forthcoming programs and events (such as the Annual Folk Life Festival, Christmas Sing, and Carnival). The visitor center is open daily, from 8:00 a.m. to 4:30 p.m. Tel: (340) 776-6201 x 238. You can also find helpful information on the park website at *https://www.nps.gov/viis.*

As you depart the visitor center, find your way to the steps behind the building, which take you to the start of the Lind Point Trail. The trail goes to the Battery Overlook and on to Salomon and Honeymoon beaches. (See *Hiking Trails, #1 Lind Point Trail, p. 116,* and *Beaches, #1 Honeymoon Beach, pp. 159-160.*) It's an easy 10-minute hike to the Overlook, where the British erected a hostile battery during one of their two occupations, in either 1801 or 1807. The retaining wall for the battery is still there, but the cannons are gone. Enjoy scenic harbor views from a bench on the hilltop.

For those wishing to continue on to Salomon or Honeymoon beaches, the latter is the more popular beach for swimming. Honeymoon also offers refreshments, and there are paddle boards and kayaks for rent. Both beaches can also be accessed from the Caneel Bay Resort as well as from the beginning of the upper Lind Point Trail at the North Shore Road intersection.

Story of Lind Point Battery

The British constructed the Lind Point Battery during the Napoleonic Wars when England and Denmark were on opposite sides of the conflict. According to local legend, the fortification was erected in a single night by troops landing secretly along the seaward side of the hill. While residents slept, soldiers worked feverishly hauling heavy cannons up the steep slope (or so the story goes). When villagers awoke the next morning, they were startled and intimidated by the presence of British guns towering above them. They quickly surrendered without a fight.

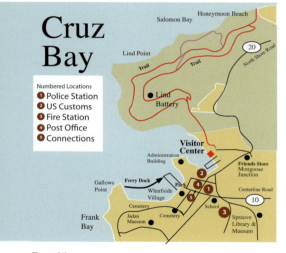

Town Map

After retracing your steps back down the trail, follow the driveway behind the visitor center out to its intersection with North Shore Road. Mongoose Junction is directly ahead. Here you'll find eateries and plenty of shopping opportunities. Take a moment to visit the Friends Store, where you can purchase handcrafted items, books, and literature about the island.

Friends of the National Park

Friends of the National Park was formed in 1988. It's a nonprofit organization that works in conjunction with the park service to help

WALKING TOUR OF CRUZ BAY   41

protect and conserve our Virgin Islands National Park. The Friends have a small paid staff that supports its 5,000 members, many of whom volunteer their time to help aid park programs and educational activities. The Friends are responsible for maintaining 27 miles of park trails through a volunteer program in which visitors can also participate. They also coordinate the ranger-guided Reef Bay and L'Esperance hiking tours and are tasked with installing hundreds of marine moorings to help protect the reefs and marine ecosystem. A brochure of classes and sponsored activities is available at the store. Typical classes include palm weaving, coastal ecology, island marine biology, West Indian cooking, and local archeology. Other programs might include hikes with local scientists, kayaking excursions, and snorkeling tours through the mangroves. For additional information call (340) 779-4940 or e-mail the Friends at *info@friendsvinp.org*. Information can also be found on the Friends website at *https://www.friendsvinp.org*. New memberships are always welcome. The Friends *Ranger Hawksbill* app is designed to assist with communicating vital information to our young visitors.

Friends of the National Park Store

The app includes a clickable map of trails and beaches with detailed descriptions of amenities. There's a "What's That?" section to help identify unique plants and animals. Safety information and park contacts are also included. The *Ranger Hawksbill* app is generally available for free in iTunes and at Google Play Store.

Leaving Mongoose

Junction, go left and continue walking along the waterfront towards the center of town. The sidewalk is usually crowded with a generous mix of locals and tourists. Arriving early in the morning, you'll find vendors selling a variety of items, including fresh produce, coconut milk, and fish.

Newcomers sometimes find it confusing and difficult and very often misleading to understand the lingo of native islanders. Their cadence is quite different, as are the meanings of many of their expressions. Local author and long-time resident Erva Boulon tells of one of her humorous encounters with the oddity of the local language, which took place while she was living on the beach at Trunk Bay:

> *While [I was] camping on the beach, George [a young local boy who helped with maintaining the house and], who was slightly scornful of this informal way of living, confronted me one fine afternoon when I came dripping out of the sea from a lovely swim and said, "Madam, shall I catch the fire?" I had visions of George darting after a fleeing flame until I realized he was asking about lighting the fire!* - (**My Island Kitchen**, **By Erva Boulon, Section 2.**)

Reaching Droningens Gade (at the post office), turn right. At the end of the road sits a large, white structure originally known as the "Battery," which is today more often referred to as the "Administration Building."

Administration ("Battery") Building

Following the Revolt of 1733, the fearful planters agreed that a battery must be built in Cruz Bay as a defense against future uprisings. The original Fortsberg stronghold at Coral Bay was destroyed after the revolt, and there was apprehension that there could be future rebellions. The ultimate location as to where the battery should be built was a controversial issue. In 1737 the Danish Crown purchased land on what is currently Gallows Point with the intention of building the battery there. Work failed to commence immediately, and the land lay idle for years. When von Rohr was completing his survey of the town in 1766, he strongly favored

WALKING TOUR OF CRUZ BAY

Gallows Point as the best spot for a battery. However, Governor Peter Clausen ignored von Rohr's recommendation, and in 1774 he had the battery built at its present-day location. Von Rohr and others felt the inner-harbor location of the present building afforded poor visibility of approaching vessels.

The structure was originally known as "Fort Christian," but its name was later officially changed to the "Battery." Several of St. John's administrators have lived here, hence its frequent reference as the "Administration Building." For quite a few years, the St. John administrator was also the local doctor. Many enjoyed this arrangement. Because the administrator's governing duties generally kept him busy at the fort, everyone knew where to find the doctor in a medical emergency. In 1946 George Simmons became the first Virgin Islands, African-American appointed administrator, who also lived at the "Battery."

Gun Platform, Battery Building

Over time the building was modified and altered to accommodate several uses — courthouse, jail, hospital, and police headquarters. Despite modifications, the architectural style of the building has retained much of its original colonial Danish character.

Adding the courthouse in 1825 was seen by some as a hopeful sign that perhaps justice for enslaved laborers would no longer be determined solely by planters, but rather by an impartial judicial body.

If you walk up to the building and peer through the gates, you'll notice a couple of cannons still in place. There is a plaque on the wall inside the courtyard bearing a partially legible epitaph to James Wright, who oversaw construction of the premise. The meritorious inscription reads as follows:

> Constructed by Freedman James Wright, born on St. John who thereafter earned his freedom with the enterprise and good be-

*havior which gained his superiors favor and his fellow citizens'
respect among whom he holds the position of first lieutenant in
the Brigade on St. Thomas, 1825.*

James Wright was an important person in his time. Born enslaved in 1775, he bought his freedom around 1796 through hard work and wages earned as a carpenter. He was a staunch advocate for the civil rights of his people during a time when no former enslaved people held positions of trust under the Danish Crown. In 1816 he boldly signed The Freedman Petition, which, while it went mostly unaddressed, was significant as one of the first formal attempts by oppressed members of the population to present a formal list of grievances directly to the Danish King. Returning to the main road, turn right. Just opposite the entrance to the ferry landing you'll reach the village park.

Franklin A. Powell, Sr. Park

The park and its immediate area trace their history to Danish colonial times when this location was referred to as "Kings Landing." It was used as a parade ground for Danish military detachments as well as a departure point for boat passengers and cargo (much like today). The dock was probably originally constructed in the mid-nineteenth century. At certain times of the year, mostly on Saturdays, vendors set up booths in the park. It's an excellent opportunity to sample local cuisine and fresh produce.

The statue in the center of the park commemorates the historic rebellion that began on November 23, 1733. It depicts the upper half of a formidable man blowing into a conch-shell horn, alerting other captives that the revolt had begun.

The event began in Coral Bay at Fortsberg where a lone, unsuspecting sentry in the early morning dawn granted access to a small group of Akwamu laborers carrying bundles of firewood. Once inside the fort, the men withdrew cane knives that had been disguised in their piles of wood. They quickly overpowered and killed the guard. Others who had been hiding in the bush streamed in and killed five of the remaining soldiers who were mostly half asleep and only semiconscious following a late night of heavy drinking.

WALKING TOUR OF CRUZ BAY

Rebel with a Conch

One guard (Jan Gabriel) escaped by hiding under a bunk and was able to make his way to St. Thomas where he delivered the alarming news of the insurrection. After ransacking the fort, the rebels mounted the gun deck and fired two cannon blasts, thus signaling the start of the revolt. Using drums and conch-shell horns, others spread the word. After confiscating anything of value, the rebels left the fort and embarked on an island-wide rampage. At nearby Estate Caroline, a planter and leading magistrate named John Sodtmann was among the first to perish along with his twelve-year-old stepdaughter.

Once news of the insurgency reached St. Thomas, the Danes sent troops to quell the rebellion. However, order was not easily restored. This was a successful, well-planned revolt, which courageous rebels managed to perpetuate for seven months despite overwhelming odds. When it was over, nearly half of the plantations were destroyed.

Nazareth Lutheran Church

To the right of the park and across from Connections, look for a white church with a small courtyard in front. The Nazareth Lutheran Church was constructed in 1958 on land formerly occupied by a Lutheran chapel and Sunday school. The architecture is representative of the early transfer years, with some touches of colonial Danish influence. The church doors are usually open to visitors, offering an invitingly cool place to pause and reflect. The Lutheran religion was the State religion of Denmark. The date "1720" above the church door commemorates the formation of the congregation, but it was not until a few years later that the first Nazareth Lutheran Church was actually built.

Missionaries played an important role in the daily life of the enslaved population. Lutherans and Moravians began sending missionaries to the Virgin Islands in 1732. They built churches, taught, and held religious gatherings, which the enslaved laborers were permitted to attend. Although the Lutheran Church was the State Church, their unbending requirement that all converts for baptism first learn the Danish language, caused more converts to join the Moravian church than the Lutheran. Eventually, Anglicans, Dutch Reformed, Catholics, Jews, and other denominations were also allowed to build places of worship on St. John.

In 1721, the Lutheran minister, Pastor Jacob Tamdrup, brought the congregation a silver chalice and paten from Denmark. These sacred communion vessels have been in continuous use by the congregation since 1723. The baptismal font is made of St. Thomas mahogany and is more than 100 years old.

Leaving the church, follow the road back towards the ferry dock. You'll be turning left onto Strand Gade, which runs adjacent to Wharfside Village. But first pause for a moment. While standing at the Strand Gade intersection, note the corner building to your immediate left. Architecturally, although the roof design and second floor have been modified, the structure still retains some of its colonial Danish character and probably dates to the early 1800s when a store existed at this location. The building once housed the iconic Mooie's Rum Shop owned by Theovald E. Moorehead, a native St. Johnian with a deep

Nazareth Lutheran Church

commitment to community betterment. Mooie was a hard-working businessman, who served as a senator in the Virgin Islands Legislature from 1957 to 1970. He was a staunch advocate of self-determination, local control of the economy, and protection of native land rights. In 1955, when the federal government and Laurance Rockefeller were discussing plans to relocate the native population to make way for the coming of the Virgin Islands National Park, he became outraged. He abandoned his military career, and moved back home to St. John to help lead a successful effort to defeat the plan. Moorehead was upset at the national park and Rockefeller for even considering such a plan, but he was equally angry with those native St. Johnians who were apparently willing to sell their heritage for material gain. Moorehead was a visionary who wanted to make it possible for native St. Johnians to benefit from what he sensed would become a booming tourist industry. As a senator, he teamed up with a former senator, Julius E. Sprauve, Sr., and three prominent locals, Albert Sewer, Ronald A. Morrisette, Sr., and Loredon Boynes Sr., to create the St. John Development Corporation. The initial goal of the corporation was to provide dependable ferry service between St. John and St. Thomas. Moorehead projected that revenues from stock sales could also be used to build tourist-related businesses such as restaurants, boat yards, and hotels. Profits would accrue to shareholders, who would be native people from St. John.

Albert Sewer was a local entrepreneur whose work ethic, ingenuity, and self-motivation closely mirrored what Mooie espoused. Albert ran a well-stocked emporium on the next block over from Mooie's Rum Shop, known back then as Sewer's Cut-Rate Store and the best place in town where one could buy big cakes of ice (a prized commodity), and only at two cents a pound! Albert stocked "every kind of sundry from kitchen utensils to jewelry," observed author George Eggleston after visiting his store during a brief stopover while cruising the Windward Islands with his wife in 1956:

> *The surprising part of his operation,* Eggleston noted, *is a small annex built on the back where several women operate sewing machines. Albert went to New York for training in the garment district and now is the Christian Dior of the outer islands. He de-*

signs all kinds of dresses and fancy blouses and shorts for women and personally sells his creations as far south as St. Kitts. He imports his fabrics from New York and even produces wedding gowns from his own designs.... The emporium handles very little apparel for men. Albert frankly explains why he specializes in women's things rather than men's:

"The man, he never has money for hisself. He always have two women to buy for, his wife an his lady frein'. So, I concentrates only on the female market an' sell twice as much stuff as otherwise." - **(George T. Eggleston, Virgin Islands, p. 30, reproduced with special permission of Krieger Publishing and members of the Eggleston family.) George Eggleston was a leading spokesman in the heated debate leading up to World War II over U.S. entry into the conflict. After the Japanese attack on Pearl Harbor, Eggleston gave his full support to the U.S. war effort, and he enlisted in the U.S. Navy. Following the war, Eggleston worked for Life Magazine, edited Scribner's Commentator, and was an editor at Reader's Digest. He authored several books about boats, tropical islands, and Christian teachings.**

Take a few minutes to visit some of the Wharfside Village shops, including St. John Spice, easily distinguished by the enticing aromas it emits to the street below. This charming, second-story shop is located at the top of the steps facing the entrance to the public ferry dock. It features a wide selection of island spices and gift items along with a nice assortment of books and other information about St. John. It's not to be missed!

Leaving Wharfside Village, continue up Strand Gade and turn right at the next intersection. Follow the road along the waterfront, heading towards Gallows Point. The peninsula is so named because individuals accused of crimes were said to have once been executed here. Nowadays, Gallows Point is home to the town cemetery. Many graves are quite old. Some are constructed of stones and others with concrete blocks built above ground to protect the interned souls from the high-water table. In the old days, conch shells were often placed on island graves to guard the deceased from evil spirits (a custom still practiced by some).

More Notable Locals

The cemetery is another quiet spot to pause and reflect on a few more personalities who left lasting impressions on present-day St.

John. Some are buried here. Others rest peacefully at different cemeteries or grave sites around the island.

Carl Francis (1867-1936)

Carl Emanuel Francis was a notable St. John figure whose parents, George Francis and Lucy Blyden, were both former enslaved persons. His father was an extremely well-regarded man who, through hard labor, eventually became the owner of Annaberg and Mary Point. George died when Carl was only eight. Carl worked hard along with his siblings and mother trying to keep things going. But economic conditions were extremely harsh, and the family fell into poverty and lost most of its property, including Annaberg. Carl did not give up. Instead he moved to Santo Domingo, where he lived and worked diligently for many years, eventually saving enough money to repurchase Annaberg and most of the other family property that had been lost. Upon his return to St. John, Carl married Amy Elizabeth Penn. The couple lived and raised their family at Annaberg. Carl managed to support his family with farming and animal husbandry, and was a successful cattle dealer. Over the years, Carl Francis became a prominent and respected figure. He served as the St. John representative to the Colonial Council and lay reader for the Nazareth Lutheran congregation in Cruz Bay. In recognition of his community dedication, he was given the honor of raising the first United States flag over St. John in the transfer ceremonies held at the Cruz Bay Battery on April 15, 1917. Carl was early on recognized and applauded as a strong and outspoken advocate for numerous causes aimed at the betterment of the local population. - **(Information from** *St. John Tradewinds,* **"Carl Emanuel Francis: Cattle Dealer to Councilman,"** https://stjohntradewinds.com/carl-emanuel-francis-from-cattle-dealer-to-councilman/.**)**

Carl Francis, Courtesy https://the-sacredalchemist.tripod.com, *photographer unknown*

Doris and Ivan Jadan

Doris and her beloved husband Ivan were well-known residents who lived happily on St. John for forty years. Before Ivan and Doris met, Ivan was an accomplished Russian tenor. Like many Russian artists of the World War II era, Ivan found it difficult to freely practice his religious beliefs and to express his artistic talents in Soviet Russia. In 1941 he managed a harrowing escape from the USSR, accompanied by his then wife Olga and son, along with fellow artists from the Bolshoi Theater. Ivan eventually made his way to St. John and subsequently discovered the freedom that he had prayed God would help him find.

Doris was born in Tuscaloosa, Alabama. She first heard Ivan sing while visiting the town of Wilhelm, Germany in 1947. Doris was immediately attracted to the sound of his voice. The two met, and a friendship developed.

Through family connections, Doris was able to bring Ivan and his family to New York, where Doris and Ivan began seeing each other regularly. After living secretly together for a time, and fearing that at any moment the KGB would find them and forcibly repatriate Ivan, the couple moved to Tampa, where they took comfort in sequestering themselves in the city's large and growing community of Russian expats. By this time, Ivan was once again single, and he and Doris were married in Tampa in 1951. The newlyweds arrived on St. John while on a cruise in 1955. It was Doris's thirtieth birthday. Even before stepping ashore, Ivan instantly announced to Doris that this was where he belonged and where he would stay, and he meant it.

Doris and Ivan occupied a small house on the hilltop above Gallows Point. Doris worked as a school teacher, and Ivan found employment at the Caneel Bay Resort. Frequent visitors and dinner guests included notable figures like Robert and Kitty Oppenheimer, with whom they developed a deep and lasting kinship. There were also memorable family visits with nieces, nephews, and siblings. Nephew Clay Hiles recalls vividly his numerous diving adventures in Frank Bay with Ivan in search of Ivan's "pet octopus." His sister, Leslie Paoletti, fondly remembers once greeting her flamboyant aunt aboard a cruise ship on which Doris was a passenger, when it docked in New York. Upon opening her cabin door, a laughing Doris gleefully met her surprised niece with a hand of bananas perched precariously on her head.

After Ivan passed away, Doris maintained a museum in his honor at their hilltop home. The museum is open to the public by request. It is generally kept locked, but the caretaker lives on the property in the small log house. Unless otherwise committed, he is happy to take you through the museum. *(See Cruz Bay town map, p. 40, for location.)*

Doris was a dedicated educator and was very active in the St. John community. She started the Virgin Islands Environmental Studies Program at Julius E. Sprauve School and authored six books, including the 1985 publication *A Guide to the Natural History of St. John*; several cookbooks; and literary works about her husband. She was also a newspaper columnist writing articles from time-to-time for the *V.I. Daily News, Tradewinds,* and *St. John Times.*

Doris was a truly colorful person always in pursuit of one cause or another. Long-time friend, June Barlas, recalls the time that Doris jumped fully clothed off the *Jolly Roger* ferry to show students while on a school field trip how legendary resident Ethel McCully made her initial arrival at Maho Bay. On another occasion Doris called reporters together to complain about the local police department giving her a rough time about trying to register her golf cart as a car. She eventually managed to gather 700 signatures supporting her petition to register the cart. The police finally relented. In the

Jadan Graves

years to follow, she became a familiar sight driving her cart around Cruz Bay with her dog Pushkin by her side.

Both Ivan and Doris are buried in the Cruz Bay cemetery. Their graves are marked by the iconic Russian Orthodox cross. - **(Parts of this information are courtesy of** *"The St. Thomas Source,"* https://stthomassource.com/content/2004/12/21/educator-author-and-community-activist-jadan-dies/ **with contributions from members of the Jadan family.)**

Miss Lucy

Lucy-Smith Prince, known locally as "Miss Lucy," was one of St. John's few early female taxi drivers. She was fondly known for her frequent wearing of a hibiscus in her hair. Her colorful taxi was distinguished by a memorable set of goat horns decorated with

Miss Lucy, Original Photographer Unknown

flowers that she proudly displayed on the cab's hood. Visitors recalled her colorful commentary and came back looking for Miss Lucy, year after year. She was a true entrepreneur who got her early start in business from selling bread, pastries, and drinks from her home in Fris Bay. Miss Lucy was a staunch supporter of local events. Her favorites included the Fourth of July celebration, Coral Bay Labor Day Parade, and the annual Christmas Sing at the basketball court. She had a reputation for being an independent thinker who was always ready to help others. In 2004, the St. John Festival and Cultural Committee recognized Miss Lucy's spirit, self-attained accomplishments, and community commitment by naming the Fourth of July celebration village in her honor. Her popular waterfront eatery in Calabash Boom called "Miss Lucy's," was legendary for being the go-to destination for the best "Sunday brunch." Miss Lucy passed away in 2007 at the age of ninety-one. She was a bigger-than-life lady who is still fondly remembered today for her many contributions to tourism, her love of St. John's natural beauty, and as one who cared deeply for her fellow island residents. - **(Information taken from** *The St. Thomas Source*, **"St. John Mourns Miss Lucy, World Famous Taxi Driver and Restauranteur,"** *https://stthomassource.com/content/2007/10/03/st-john-mourns-miss-lucy-world-famous-taxi-driver-and-restaurateur.)*

Guy Benjamin

Born October 18, 1913, Guy Benjamin was a passionate educator and the first St. John local to graduate from high school. In June 1974, the Virgin Islands Legislature approved Resolution 714 in recognition of his more than forty years of "distinguished and faithful service to the people of the Virgin Islands as an out-

WALKING TOUR OF CRUZ BAY   53

standing leader and educator." Benjamin earned a B.A. degree in English from Howard University in Washington, D.C. followed by an M.A. in school administration from NYU. During his years as a teacher, he worked hard to make ferry service between St. John and St. Thomas possible so that children on his island could have the opportunity to attend school past the sixth grade. Before ferry service was initiated, parents were forced to board their children on St. Thomas, an expense few could afford. A former school in Coral Bay was named in Benjamin's honor. Benjamin was passionate about promoting equality among races and respect for each other's ways. He was extremely proud when referring to the election of President Barack Obama, our nation's first black president. "I have seen the impossible happen," he told fellow Rotarians at a 2009 meeting, "the impossible dream has become a reality." Benjamin openly espoused the opportunity our nation afforded. The United States, he believed, was "the only place in the world where anyone can be anything they want to be if they have the ability."

Benjamin wrote two books - *Me and My Beloved Virgin* and *More Tales from Me and My Beloved Virgin*. To the many who knew him, Benjamin was a renowned educator and scholar, but also a true gentleman and friend who touched many lives during his time on earth. He died in 2012 at the age of ninety-eight.

- (Textual information courtesy of *The St. Thomas Source*, "Guy Benjamin Dies at Age 98," https://stthomassource.com/content/2012/06/20/guy-benjamin-dies-age-98/.)

Guy Benjamin, Courtesy https://www.proprofs.com, photographer unknown

Julius E. Sprauve, Sr. (1892-1965)

Julius Sprauve served twenty years on the St. Thomas Municipal Council and became the first popularly elected senator from St. John to serve in the Virgin Islands Legislature. During his many years as a senator, his primary goal was always to improve social and economic conditions on St. John, especially for native St. Johnians.

One of his many outstanding achievements includes his successful effort to create affordable housing opportunities for islanders.

> *"His greatest accomplishment was the Homestead Act,"* notes his son, Elroy Sprauve. *"[My] father convinced people who owned large tracts of land in the Enighed and Contant areas to sell to the local government,"* Elroy said. *In turn, the government sold lots at $19 each to residents who otherwise wouldn't be able to afford them. Five-acre parcels went for $125.*

Other key concerns for which he sponsored legislation included road improvements, improved and increased water storage facilities, expanded healthcare access, a new school, and extended welfare services. He was an environmentalist, who was passionately interested in protecting the natural beauty of the island from the onslaught of commercialism. When opposition to a bill calling for the creation of the Virgin Islands National Park surfaced in Congress, Sprauve wrote a letter in defense of the park, which proved persuasive in promoting the bill's passage. - **(Information and quotation provided by** *The St. Croix Source,* *https://stcroixsource.com/2008/02/14/black-history-spotlight-julius-e-sprauve/***.)**

Moving On

A few steps beyond the commissary at Gallows Point, the road drops down to the shore of Frank Bay. The beach is open to the public. It's a favorite swimming and snorkeling spot for in-town residents. Most evenings, residents and visitors alike gather here to

WALKING TOUR OF CRUZ BAY

55

watch the sunset.

The beach is known for good snorkeling and frequent sightings of small octopuses under and around the coral heads fringing the shore. While at Frank Bay, you might want to take a few minutes to visit Coconut Coast Studios, where you can purchase St. John postcards, calendars, and watercolors painted by Elaine E. Estern, who resides above her studio. During certain times of the year, Coconut Coast hosts a weekly cocktail party with music. Call (340) 776-6944 for times and dates or visit their website: *https://www. coconutcoaststudios.com.*

The Coconut Coast studio/house was built in 1947 by Cora Petit, who came here to retire along with a friend from New York, Janine Bostick, who built the house next door. Cora Petit was the grandmother of Aimery Caron of St. Thomas (whose parents owned and operated C & M Caron, a well-known Main Street gift shop) and whose sister is Leslie Caron (the renowned French-American actress). Leslie came to Hollywood from France in 1950 with her mother, Margaret Petit Caron, to film *An American in Paris.* On her way back to Paris, Margaret visited her mother Cora Petit on St. John. Margaret was so enchanted with the island and Cora Petit's little house that upon her return to Paris, she convinced her husband Claude Caron and her son Aimery that they should move to the Virgin Islands and start a new life as they (like others in Europe at the time) were still painfully recovering from the miseries of World War II. Margaret correctly sensed that the USVI was about to become a tourist mecca and that there would be a strong demand for French and European luxury products, which became a focus of the family business on St. Thomas. At Margaret's urging, they all applied for green cards (permanent residency cards), and Aimery and his mother packed their belongings and sailed to St. Thomas, arriving in January 1951. Claude Caron arrived 6-9 months later after settling business affairs in France.

Leslie Caron first came to St. John on her honeymoon after marrying Geordie Hormel in Las Vegas in 1952. Besides her film debut in the musical *An American in Paris,* she is best known for the musical films *Lili (1953), Daddy Long Legs* (1955), and *Gigi* (1958), and for the nonmusical films *Fanny* (1961), *The L-Shaped Room* (1962), and *Father Goose* (1964). She is one of the few dancers and actresses who have danced with all of the great dancers: Gene Kelly, Fred Astaire, Mikhail Baryshnikov, and Rudolf Nureyev.

Leslie held a green card from 1950 until 2007 when she finally decided to claim her American citizenship through her American born mother. She did this for the sole purpose of wanting to vote for Barack Obama.

Aimery left St. Thomas and joined his sister Leslie in Hollywood in the spring of 1951 where he earned his B.S., M.A., and Ph.D. degrees in chemistry from UCLA and USC. After several years teaching and doing research in Los Angles and Massachu-

Frank Bay Beach

setts, Aimery returned to St. Thomas in 1968. Shortly thereafter, he joined the faculty at the College (now University) of the Virgin Islands as an associate professor of chemistry, retiring in 2002 with the status of professor emeritus.

Leslie used to visit her brother Aimery and his family at their home on St. Thomas every two years during the Christmas holidays. Each time, they would take her on a tour of St. John, which of course included a stop at Coconut Coast Studios named after coconut trees planted there by their American grandmother. On New Year's Day 2017, her family took her to the Caneel Bay buffet, which she found to be perfect!

Leaving Frank Bay retrace your steps and walk back toward the intersection at Strand Gade (Catholic Church on the corner), where you earlier made a turn toward Gallows Point. Just before reaching the intersection, look to your right for a concrete driveway leading up the hillside.

The driveway takes you to the recently restored historic Martin–van Beverhoudt Family Plot. The cemetery is situated on the hillside behind the restaurant. Occupants include Sarah Elizabeth Martin and her descendants. The only other identified occupant of the six graves is Anna Louisa van Beverhoudt, who died in 1879 and was the daughter of Sarah Martin and her husband, Peter van Beverhoudt.

According to the plaque at the edge of the cemetery, Sarah obtained her freedom at approximately twenty-two years of age, during a time when she was in a relationship with Peter van Beverhoudt, a local planter and militia captain. Together, they had eleven children, all of whom were recognized by their father and carried the van Beverhoudt name.

The Martin–van Beverhoudt Family Plot is a key historical site in the history of the island. While these graves enshrine the remains of a family group bonded by blood, this notably important cemetery also connects St. John residents and visitors to a pivotal time in the history of this tiny town. Sarah Martin and her descendants were part of a dynamic and complicated community that included both enslaved and free members of African descent as well as European immigrants, plantation managers, and their descendants.

The initiative to restore the previously neglected cemetery by David W. Knight, Sr. and the St. John Historical Society was made possible through a grant from the Virgin Islands Historic Preservation Office, the efforts of volunteers from the St. John Historical

Society along with craftsmen from St. John Stone Masonry, as well as from community donations.
– (Information about this cemetery is taken partially from the plaque as well as from the research and writings of David W. Knight, Sr. and the St. John Historical Society and its members.)

The Martin–van Beverhoudt Family Plot

Continuing on, when you reach Strand Gade, do not turn left. Keep following the road straight ahead. At the turn just past the Fish Trap restaurant, the road becomes Kongens Gade and takes you to its intersection with Prindsen Gade. Here you'll find local produce and other delights often being sold at the stand in front of Connections.

For those readers wanting to proceed to the Elaine Sprauve Library, the last stop on the tour (an additional 10-minute walk), turn right at this intersection and continue walking uphill passing the Legislature Building and the police station, both on your left.

For others this may be a convenient spot to pause and take a break before going on to the library. If you're getting hungry, try sampling some of the local cuisine available at a few of the nearby intown eateries.

Local Cuisine

West Indian dishes are a mixture of African and European heritage with a large dousing of good old-fashioned imagination thrown in. Some local dishes were passed down from plantation days. Sweet potatoes, yams, pumpkins (yellow squash), peas, fish, turtles, whelks, conchs, and livestock formed the basic diet of early inhabitants. Traditional native foods are Johnnycakes (fried bread), fungi (a corn meal and okra preparation), pate (a dumpling filled with spicy meat or fish), kallaloo (a spicy combination of boiled fish and local greens), fish chowder, whole fried fish, and chicken with rice. Popular desserts are grated coconut and sugar cakes, sliced mangoes, and soursop ice cream.

Picking Up the Trail

To reach the library from the produce stand head up the road towards the rotary. The land at the corner adjacent to the rotary had traditionally been used for local concerts and holiday venues such as the St. John Festival Village (June and July), an annual event associated with the celebration of Carnival.

Carnival is part of a thirty-day occurrence commencing in early June and culminating with the July Fourth celebration of Cultural Day. The event features bike races, calypso shows, parades, and fireworks. The celebration period encompasses Organic Act Day (third Monday in June), Carnival, and Emancipation Day (July 3rd).

Carnival has its origins in plantation times, although St. John did not officially celebrate its first Carnival until 1928. Originally Carnival was devised as a form of entertainment for the local populous. It coincided with Christian Easter celebrations. As part of the festivities, enslaved captives donned costumes and mimicked their plantation owners through song and dance.

The traditional figure associated with Carnival is the moko jumbie (also known as "moko jumbi" or "mocko jumbie"). A moko jumbie is a stilts walker or dancer. "Moko" means "healer" in central African dialect and "jumbi" is a West Indian term for a ghost or spirit. Moko in the traditional sense is a god. He watches over his village, and due to his heavenly height, he is able to foresee danger and evil. The name "moko," literally means "diviner" and is represented today by men on towering stilts who perform acts that are inexplicable to the human eye. A moko jumbie character typically wears colorful garb and masks.

Locally, Willard John and his wife, Curliss Solomon-John, have been passionately involved with the evolution of their moko jumbi performing troupe, the *Guardians of Culture Moko Jumbies*. Willard was given his first pair of stilts by his cousin and was introduced to the art of stilts dancing in 1974. A year later, he danced in his first parade. "It was an exciting and spiritual experience, which still gives me that connection to my ancestors," says Willard. "I feel it when I go on those stilts forty-something years later. The height of the moko jumbie's stilts represents the powers of God," John explains:

> "They were symbolically the spiritual guardians of the village. They would protect the village from the evil spirits. Christians and Catholics make the sign of the cross and use holy water and other rituals, which mimic the origins of Africa," he said. "When Africans were enslaved and brought to this part of the world, we brought our culture with us, but it had to change to survive through…[enslavement]. The …[plantation] owners did not allow Africans to practice their culture, so the practice of mocko jumbie and other cultural practices changed as a means of celebration or festivity to be accepted"

Mocko Jumbie, Willard John, Courtesy "The St. John Source," https://stjohnsource.com/2019/03/01/the-evolution-of-the-mocko-jumbie-in-the-v-i/

"The dancers get a new costume every year. We try to come up with different ideas and different themes," says Willard's wife, Solomon-John. She makes the costumes and masks and she and Willard make the headpieces from scratch. "I've come up with a rectangular mask that will cover the face except for the eyes," she explains. "It allows them to breathe easily, yet it keeps the mysticism in their appearance."

In 2009 the Department of Tourism of the U.S. Virgin Islands adopted the moko jumbie as a symbol for the islands. – **(Information and quotation are courtesy of** *The St. John Source*, **"The Evolution of the Mocko Jumbie in the V.I.,"** *https://stjohnsource.com/2019/03/01/the-evolution-of-the-mocko-jumbie-in-the-v-i/.)*

Moving Along

Stay to the right side of the rotary, and then take the second right halfway around the circle. Keep walking. A little further ahead you'll pass by St. Ursula's Church. Take the next right. The library is on your left at the end of this short road. Before reaching the library, you come to the local Animal Care Center (ACC), which is always looking for volunteers to contribute their time while on island. For more information call (340) 774-1625. Visit their website at: *https://www.stjohnanimalcarecenter.org*. You may email them at *info@atjacc.org*.

Elaine Sprauve Library

The Elaine Ione Sprauve Library is housed in what was previously called the "Enighed Estate House," once part of a larger estate, tracing its roots to William Wood, an early colonial planter, who migrated here from Saba in the Dutch West Indies. Sometime between 1750 and 1757, Wood acquired two struggling cotton plantations at this Cruz Bay Quarter location and merged them to create a single estate.

William Wood died on his plantation in the spring of 1757, leaving his wife, Elizabeth, and their children as heirs. In 1791, Enighed was acquired by George Hassel, and in 1798 title passed to Johannes Wood, son of William and Elizabeth Wood. During the ownerships of George Hassel and Johannes Wood, Enighed became a major sugar plantation, totaling 225 acres – half of which were planted in sugar. After Johannes Wood's death in 1803, things began to deteriorate, and his heirs were eventually forced to sell the property to Guert de Windt in public auction in 1821. Things improved somewhat after two brothers – Ernst Weinmar and Peter Weinmar later acquired the property and expanded the acreage to accommodate more sugar and provision production. However, following Emancipation in 1848, the property became less and less profitable, and the mortgage was eventually foreclosed upon by the Danish government. A succession of ownerships followed. By 1880 sugar production ceased entirely. Attempts were made to revive the property by focusing on cattle raising and the export of provisions, but these efforts proved largely unprofitable. Eventually parcels of Enighed were sold off to various owners (with little or no interest in farming), until the remainder was eventually purchased by the Virgin Islands government in 1944.

William Wood's grave alongside eleven other burials in the Estate Enighed Cemetery is located near the southeast corner of the library building. It is the only remaining identifiable burial.

The inscription on Wood's gravestone reads in both Dutch and Danish and is translated as follows:

William Wood/First Alderman of the community of Jesus Christ/ Former Burger Captain of St. John/Born on Saba 22 March 1692/ Died St. John 9 March 1757.On Saba rose his sun of life, Wood, who knew God's community, His life's sun waned on St. John. Here resteh his remains. He will find the Alderman's Wages of Grace with Haven's Lord. J.IT invent et fecit

Elaine Sprauve Library

The history of the current Enighed Estate House, which is now the Elaine Sprauve Library, is a bit murky. However, most of what we see here today was probably a rebuild and enlargement by Ernst and Peter Weinman of the original Wood family house. In 1976 the Enighed Estate House was placed on the Historic Register and, in 1982, after four years of labor, the exterior of the structure was restored, and the building was outfitted for its present-day use as a library. It was named after Elaine Ione Sprauve in recognition of her achievements in government, her dedication to others, and love of her community.

The library is open Monday-Friday, 9:00 a.m. to 5:00 p.m. It closes for one hour at noon for lunch. There is free internet. For more information go to *http://www.virginislandspubliclibraries.org* or email the library at *stjohnlibraryfriends@gmail.com.*

End of Walking Tour

North Shore Motor Tour
(2.0 Hours, Approx.)

This tour takes you to historic ruins of several sugar plantations, including a self-guided walking tour of Annaberg, bay rum stills, and a colonial schoolhouse. You also visit historic ruins of the Cinnamon Bay sugar works where you will enjoy a pleasant woodland stroll and learn about local flora and fauna. The beaches along the north side of the island are gorgeous. You'll have plenty of opportunities to stop for a refreshing swim. You may want to pack a picnic lunch! The tour begins at the entrance to Caneel Bay Plantation on North Shore Road (Route 20), a little less than a mile from Cruz Bay. The resort is located within the park boundary. It is operated by a private company under a long-term lease. Caneel suffered extensive damage from hurricanes Irma and Maria in the fall of 2017 and was forced to close. When operating, certain areas of the resort including most of the restaurants, gift shop, and beach in front of the main hotel building are open to the public. There is shuttle service that takes visitors from Caneel to popular Honeymoon Beach. *(See #1 Honeymoon Beach, pp. 159-160.)*

Caneel Bay Plantation

The resort was first opened in the 1930s as a small hotel owned and operated by the West Indian Company. It was purchased by Laurance Rockefeller shortly after his initial visit in 1952, and it underwent extensive enlargement and improvement, transforming it into a premier world-renowned luxury resort.

Directly across the road from the pedestrian exit at the far end of the parking lot are the remains of the original Duurloo sugar works, including the horsemill and sugar factory.

Duurloo played a dramatic role in the story of the Revolt of 1733. Here a small group of planters, fearing for their lives, gathered in the early morning hours of the rebellion to defend themselves. The following are partial excerpts taken from an 1888 retelling of the event by C. E. Taylor, a then member of the Colonial

Ruins of Duurloo Sugar Factory

Council of St. Thomas and St. John:

Alarmed by the guns, and seeing the commotion among the… [rebels], several planters, headed by John Beverhout, with their families, rushed to the estate of Mr. Durlo, now "Little Cinnamon Bay;" the house on this estate being on an eminence, and protected by two cannons. In the meantime, a fearful sacrifice of life was taking place on some estates….

The planters who had fled to the Durlo estate, immediately dispatched a boat with a letter to the Governor of St. Thomas informing him of the insurrection, and entreating assistance at once, and deliverance from their imminent peril….The consternation and grief produced by this letter…was great….Vessels were at once dispatched to bring off survivors. By this time the …[rebels] had surrounded the eminence upon which the mansion at Durlo estate was located; and they were only repulsed by the heroic conduct…of the planters…[who] poured down upon the conspirators…a destructive fire from the two cannons, killing and wounding many. This forced them to withdraw to the foot of the hill, and, under cover of the cannons, the planters were enabled to embark their wives and children for St. Thomas and Tortola, on board the vessels which had now arrived for their assistance. – **(C.E. Taylor,** *Leaflets from the Danish West Indies,* **pp. 99-103 PD-1923.)**

NORTH SHORE MOTOR TOUR

Departing Caneel, continue driving east along North Shore Road. A short distance ahead is Hawksnest Beach, the first of several popular beaches on the route. Traveling past Hawksnest and going a bit further you come to a white picket fence followed by a metal-gated entryway. The path leads downward to a second popular beach, Gibney-Oppenheimer.

Gibney-Oppenheimer Families and Beach

This beach is named in part after Robert Oppenheimer, the well-known American theoretical physicist best remembered as the "father of the atomic bomb." The entire 40-acre beachfront property was acquired in 1950 by former New York City residents, Robert Gibney and his wife, Nancy Flagg Gibney. Robert was a writer-artist; Nancy was a magazine editor. The couple came to St. John on their honeymoon in 1946. They planned on staying only a few months, but months led to years, and eventually their beloved island became their permanent residence. Robert and Nancy managed to build their home on the beach before cars or electricity came to St. John. Here they raised and home-schooled their three children – Ed, Eleanor, and John.

The original 40-acre parcel of land purchased by the Gibneys has been divided and sold in several ways throughout the years. Some of the beach area is now part of the Virgin Islands National Park. A small piece of land on the beach was sold in 1957 by the Gibneys to Robert and Kitty Oppenheimer. This land was eventually willed to "the people of Saint John" by the Oppenheimers' daughter, Toni, after her death by suicide in 1977. Eventually, to ensure proper maintenance, the property was ultimately taken over by the Virgin Islands government.

In the summer of 1959, the Oppenheimers, eager to sequester themselves from the political turmoil surrounding them at the time, spent a few months as guests of the Gibneys, while their own house was being built. Once completed, Robert and Kitty Oppenheimer occupied their beach house with their daughter, Toni. It was never a primary residence for Robert and Kitty, who managed to stay here for only a couple of months each year through the 1960s and early 1970s. However, their daughter became a full-time resident in the last year or two of her life. The building there now, which is being used as a recreational facility, is not the Oppenheimers' original structure, but it is built on the foundation of their house. Nancy Gibney shares colorful first impressions of Robert and his wife, Kitty, in her article, *Finding Out Different:*"

> *I first met the Oppenheimers in 1956, one day when I went alone up to Trunk Bay for lunch and they were on a holiday there. Robert's security clearance had been canceled two years before; I hadn't followed the case with any attention, being far more concerned at the time with infant activities than with un-American ones. I had only a dim impression that a great man had been brought low, not for his faults but for his virtues. I was curious to observe them. I saw at once that he and his wife were the most curious people, I had ever observed.... Robert looked astoundingly like Pinocchio, and he moved as jerkily as a marionette on strings. But there was nothing wooden about his manner: he exuded warmth and sympathy and courtesy along with the fumes of his famous pipe. His voice was gentle, almost inaudible, and it became softer, the more he wanted to be heard.*
> – **("Finding Out Different," Nancy Flagg Gibney,** *Five Quarters, Journal of the St. John Historical Society,* **Vol III, Issue 3, 2015.)**

During the 1950s, Robert Gibney worked at Caneel Bay Resort and later as a librarian in Cruz Bay. Nancy helped support the family as a freelance writer of short stories, appearing regularly in popular women's magazines such as *McCall's* and *Redbook*. The Gibney sale of a portion of their land to the Oppenheimers was initially thought to be of benefit to both parties. Unfortunately, the Gibneys and the two senior Oppenheimers never really got along well as neighbors. There were squabbles for about ten years.

Robert Gibney died in 1973, and Nancy followed in 1980. As for the children, John Gibney eventually sold his hilltop land; Eleanor Gibney is on a retained estate agreement with the national park; and part of Ed Gibney's share, at the far western end of the property, is now national park. Although the original Oppenheimer property and some of the original Gibney land is today under the stewardship of the park, visitors are reminded that several of Robert and Nancy Gibneys' sixteen descendants still live on the property. Visitors are asked as a courtesy to be mindful that this is their home. Remember sound often carries long distances. Loud noise can be a disturbance to area residents. Please obey park rules and regulations and remember, DRONES ARE NOT ALLOWED IN THE PARK FOR ANY PURPOSE, INCLUDING FOR RECREATION OR COMMERCE. To report possible infractions, please call Park Watch at 1-866-995-8467.

A short distance past Gibney-Oppenheimer Beach, you'll reach a large rock prominently perched at the very edge of the road. This huge stone is known locally as "Easter Rock" because its base is supposedly always found wet on Easter morning. Legend has it that the rock gets wet by somehow managing to roll itself down the hill to the water each Easter. Coincidentally, this only seems to

Trunk Bay from Overlook

happen when nobody is looking.

Just past the rock is a small parking area on the left with a path leading up to the remains of the Peace Hill sugar works (horsemill and windmill still in place). It's a short stroll to the ruins, where one can admire unobstructed panoramas of the surrounding Atlantic waters.

After Peace Hill you come to Jumbie Beach—yet another pretty stretch of white sand with good swimming and snorkeling at either end. There is generally parking available on the right side of the road, a few yards ahead of the path leading down to the beach.

The next in this string of grand beaches is world-famous Trunk Bay Beach. Just before reaching Trunk, you approach a scenic overlook offering a dramatic vista of the gorgeous beach below. It's a safe spot to stop and take pictures!

Trunk Bay is widely recognized as being one of the most beautiful beaches in the world. It is named after leatherback turtles that used to nest at this beach in large numbers. So why the name "trunk?" Apparently leatherback turtles swimming on the ocean surface were thought by some to look like floating steamer trunks, so colonial Danes started calling these turtles "trunk turtles." This, in turn, eventually led to calling this nesting ground "Trunk Bay."

Leatherbacks were once a prized food staple on merchant ships. They could be kept alive on a ship's deck for lengthy periods, thus keeping the meat fresh for consumption. The leatherback is the largest of the sea turtles, and the only one lacking a hard shell. They are typically 4 to 6 feet long and weigh 600 to 1,100 pounds. The largest leatherback ever recorded was almost 10 feet long and weighed 2,019 pounds.

Trunk Bay Beach/ Boulon Family Guest House

In 1959 the park service purchased Trunk Bay from the Boulon family who ran a successful guest house here for many years. Erva Boulon (January 8, 1895–December 27, 1972) and her guest house are legendary. So also, is Erva's cookbook, *My Island Kitchen*, published in 1969, which contains an autobiography and narrative of her island adventures. Erva's father, Frank Hartwell, was a weatherman for the Federal Weather Bureau (now the National Oceanic and Atmospheric Administration), whose duties first moved the family from Nebraska to Cuba. Later moves includ-

Erva Boulon, Courtesy of the Boulon Family

ed residences in Key West and the Dry Tortugas. In 1908 the family landed in Puerto Rico where Erva grew up. It was there she met and married Paul Boulon. The couple eventually found their way to St. John, along with four small children. They purchased Trunk Bay in 1928 and built a two-story, five-bedroom vacation home, which later evolved into their guest house. The Boulon Guest House was famous for its privacy and reputation for delicious West Indian cooking, adjusted for American tastes. Robert and Kitty Oppenheimer stayed here. Famous literary guests included novelist John Dos Pasos, most noted for his *U.S.A.* trilogy, and John Gunther, journalist and author of a series of popular sociopolitical works known as the "Inside" books, which included *Inside Africa* and *Inside U.S.A.*, and his memoir *Death Be Not Proud*, written on the death of his beloved teenage son. Other notable guests included Frances Farmer, Henry Fonda, Richard Widmark, and Jerome Robbins of *West Side Story* fame.

Erva savored the everyday excitement of her life on St. John. Even the most mundane chores like a "routine" shopping trip to the market on Tortola became an adventure:

> *A trip to Tortola, a neighboring British Island becomes a sea going picnic on our cruiser "Eve." Saturday is the best day because that is market day in Tortola. Starting at Trunk Bay you will cruise along the north shore of St. John, passing Cinnamon Bay, cutting through Whistling Cay and Mary's Point into Sir Francis Drake's Channel, a windy, narrow passage bordered by Thatch Island, a British possession, on one side, and St. John, an American possession, on the other. Deep blue water, sharp rocky cliffs, an occasional small goat leaping from rock to rock, pelicans looking very silly on their nests in the trees and the tyre*

palms giving a tropical touch.

An hour and a half from Trunk Bay you reach Road Town, the capital of Tortola. A customs official meets the boat. He is clothed in the dignity of his office, a uniform of spotless whites as he clears you for your visit ashore. This is a painless procedure which does not involve a passport.

Market is in full swing. Baskets of plantains, mangoes, avocados, gandules, bananas, etc. add as much gaiety and color to the scene as the woman's bright skirts. Along the dock, sloops bob about with the day's catch of fish, adding still more color to the scene; blue, yellow, red and silver....

Back in the thirties it was a breach of etique'te if one did not pay his respects to the resident Commissioner. The ladies must wear shirts and the gentlemen "sacks" (jackets) for this very pleasant interlude in the charming old house where the Commissioner lived. It is a pity that this courtesy has been lost over the years.

Your purchases made, you all troop back to the "Eve" for a picnic lunch. Returning to Trunk Bay at a leisurely trolling speed. On your way home you will most likely catch a kingfish or Spanish mackerel, adding excitement to the trip as well as fish for dinner. On this trip we caught a twenty-pound king. - (**My Island Kitchen**, by Erva Boulon, Section 4)

Until a few years ago, the sugar factory ruins, located directly across the road from the parking lot, were in desperate need of repair. Thankfully, in 2009 a team of restoration masons from the San Juan National Historic Site began reinforcing them. The team filled cracks in the walls using historically approved mortar and

Coral Scene, Courtesy John Dawson, NPS, PD

NORTH SHORE MOTOR TOUR

installed wooden scaffolding supports and beams to secure them.

The palm-fringed beach is excellent for sunbathing and swimming. An underwater snorkel trail offers visitors a chance to explore the reef and identify various forms of sea life with the aid of underwater signage. A variety of fish and diverse types of coral formations inhabit the reefs. Butterfish, parrot fish, and angelfish are common. Coral types include brain, staghorn, elkhorn, and sea fans. The drawing *(see p. 70)* by John Dawson illustrates the diversity of the reef inhabitants. (See *Checklist of Corals, Fish, and other Marine Life, pp. 185-196,* for common aquatic identifications.)

Cinnamon Bay

The next stop on this tour is Cinnamon Bay. Cinnamon Bay Plantation was one of the earliest sugar settlements on St. John. The campground was totally destroyed during the 2017 hurricanes and had to be temporally closed. The beach is open to the public. *(See #7 Cinnamon Bay Beach, p. 163.)*

Be sure to explore the ruins and walking trail. There's an elevated wooden walkway (handicapped accessible) that takes you through much of the former sugar works. Enjoy a self-guided hike with plaques describing local vegetation and other points of interest. On the hike you learn about animals and plants that live in the forest. (See *Hiking Trails, #5 Cinnamon Bay Loop Trail, pp. 118-126.*)

The Cinnamon Bay beachfront is the location of a major archeological dig that took place here in the early 1990s. Discoveries made here changed our understanding as to the nature of the people who lived on St. John during the 500 years leading up to the arrival of Columbus in 1493. Pieces of broken pottery provided convincing evidence that they were *classic* Tainos, who probably migrated here from Puerto Rico and Hispaniola. *Classic* Tainos were a more culturally advanced people than the less-developed *eastern* Tainos, who had previously been thought to have inhabited the area. It's believed that a temple once stood on the beach. Here villagers brought offerings for ancestral deities called "zemis," which were idols made from a variety of materials including wood, stone, and coral. Artifacts unearthed here were for a time housed in a museum on the beach, which was destroyed by the 2017 hurricanes. Efforts are underway to find a new location to display these valuable relics.

Near the path to the beach and close to the shore you'll find a stone slab with a plaque marking the common grave of former inhabitants. Its inscription solemnly reads: "Here lie the remains of individuals from Africa and Europe who lived, worked, and died here in the 17th, 18th, and 19th centuries." It's believed that some buried here were victims of the 1903 cholera epidemic.

Moving Along

As you leave Cinnamon and continue driving east, note the sign on the immediate right side of the road marking the entrance to the Cinnamon Bay Hiking Trail. This forested path follows a colonial Danish road uphill where it intersects with Centerline Road. A short distance up the trail is a connecting path that takes you to the ruins of the America Hill great house. Many of St. John's trails are actually part of the original Danish road system. During colonial times, North Shore Road did not exist. The main thoroughfare was Konge Vej. It traversed the mountaintops and ran between Cruz Bay and Coral Bay, approximating present-day Centerline Road. To reach plantations on the north and south sides of the island, trails ran down the mountain sides.

A short distance beyond Cinnamon, the road drops down and passes along the shore of Maho Bay, a favorite spot for boaters, sunbathers, and swimmers. The beach is conveniently accessed from the edge of the road at several points. There are concessions where you can rent kayaks and other water toys. You'll find a parking lot at the far east end of the beach. *(See #8 Maho Bay Beach, p. 164)*

The hilltop on the east side of the bay was for thirty-six years the site of legendary Maho Bay Camps. The camps were conceived and operated by pioneer eco-resort developer Stanley Selengut, revered by many as the "father of sustainable resort development."

The campground was built in 1976, utilizing techniques designed to limit erosion and disturbance of plants and wildlife. Tent sites were connected by wooden walkways perched above the land.

Alternative energy sources were employed wherever possible, and visitors were encouraged to recycle and reuse their consumer products. Stanley also built a sister eco-resort, Concordia, on the south side of St. John, which reopened in 2020 under new owners after suffering extensive hurricane damage. Stanley is the recipient of The International Ecotourism Society (TIES) Lifetime Achievement Award for his tireless commitment to promoting ecotourism.

Stanley Selengut (right) and Randy Koladis, White Bay Fish Fry, ca. 2009

About 0.25 miles from Maho Bay, you come to a fork in the road. Bear left. Just past the fork, look for the preserved remnant of a colonial Danish road on your right. It once connected the neighboring estates of Windberg and Frederiksdal. There is also a short path, a bit further ahead, which leads to the site of a colonial schoolhouse.

The Annaberg School is a tangible reminder of the liberal administration of Governor Peter von Scholten (1836-48), who pushed hard for the passage of compulsory education for all children. In total, seventeen von Scholten schools were built in the Virgin Islands, four of which were constructed here on St. John. The governor wanted to give enslaved laborers an opportunity for upward mobility and to prepare them for their forthcoming freedom. Prior to passage of compulsory education laws, children were generally expected to work as soon as they were old enough. There was very little time for leisure activities or play. Children were required to assist parents with work in the fields or were assigned other tasks according to age and strength. Some tasks typically performed by children included feeding livestock and gathering dried cane stalks used for fuel. "Gangs" were organized for specific tasks. Everyone, not just children, belonged to a work gang, according to ability.

When schooling was finally instituted, the hours were structured around regular work requirements of the children. Younger chil-

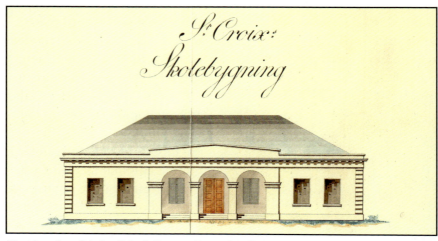

Elevation of von Scholten School, Courtesy National Archives, Denmark, PD, https://www.virgin-islands-history.org/en/history/slavery/enslaved-children-work-and-leisure-time/

dren, ages 4-8, attended school weekdays for three hours a day. Older children were expected to continue to do their full-time labor and went to school only on Saturday morning. At first, Moravian missionaries served as teachers and classes were conducted in the English language.

Construction was started and substantially completed on the Annaberg School in 1847, but the school then sat idle for a lengthy period before officially opening on August 12, 1856. Brother Gardin penned the following report to Moravian officials announcing the school's opening:

> In St. Jan we have this year opened a school at Annaberg on the north side of the island. The schoolhouse, which is in a charming situation, by the sea, was built many years ago, but never used. There are now twenty-five children in attendance. - PD-1923

Staffing the Annaberg School was difficult. When the director was dismissed for "gross immorality" in 1861, students in the area were sent to the Emmaus Moravian Station in Coral Bay, and the school never re-opened. The decision not to reopen probably had something to do with diminished need, as fewer and fewer formerly enslaved workers remained on plantations following Emancipation.

Just beyond the schoolhouse path, the road splits again. The road to the left goes to Francis Bay, which we will return to shortly. For the moment, go right and continue following the road along Leinster Bay in the direction of the Annaberg ruins.

Driving along the shore, you pass groves of poisonous manchineel trees. Avoid contact with the tree. Its leaves, bark, and tiny green "apples" contain a highly caustic sap. Early explorers recorded numerous bad experiences with this tree.

Columbus described its green fruit as "death apples" after several of his men fell critically ill from eating them. In 1526 Gonzalo Fernandez de Oviedo, writing in his *Natural History of the West Indies,* warned about the dangers of the fruit:

Dick Culbert, Courtesy Wikimedia under creative commons license, https://commons.wikimedia.org/wiki/File:Hippomane_mancinella,_the_Death_Apple_(11239909065).jpg

I say that if a man lies down to sleep for only an hour in the shade of one of these manchineel trees, he awakes with his head and eyes swollen, his eyebrows level with his cheeks. If by chance a drop of dew falls from this tree into a man's eyes, his eyes will burst, or at least the man will go blind.

The paved road ends at the entrance to the Annaberg ruins. Public parking is usually available in the paved area at the bottom of the hill. The rotary up the hill at the entrance to the ruins is reserved for public transportation.

Annaberg Sugar Works

Annaberg stands today as a reminder of a bygone age. By the 1400s, Europeans had developed a taste for sweets. At the time, sugar cane—a plant native to southern Asia—was the only known source for sugar, a fact that left Europe dependent on Asian growers as the primary suppliers of the product. When European powers saw how the plant thrived in the tropical climate and recognized its potential for trade, they raced to claim colonies in the Americas.

There were nearly 100 plantations on St. John by the early eighteenth century, but not all planters could bear the expense of growing sugar cane. Building a sugar processing facility took a great deal of money, which few could afford.

The burden of operating plantations like Annaberg fell to generations of enslaved Africans, who came to represent the bulk of the population.

The Annaberg sugar works that we see here today is an outgrowth of the former Constantin plantation, which was established by Isaac Constantin in 1721. The Constantin plantation was located on the north shore of Leinster Bay (known for many years as "Constantin Bay"). Constantin was an ambitious French Huguenot who, with his wife and young daughter, moved to St. John from St. Thomas after receiving a land grant to the property. After several years, Constantin had managed to establish a sugar works at Leinster Bay. When he died in 1732, the St. John property was inherited, along with Constantin's St. Thomas holdings, by his heirs. The St. John sugar works were damaged during the Revolt of 1733. However, they were rebuilt, and Constantin's relations continued to operate the sugar works before the property was taken over by the court when the last surviving heir passed away.

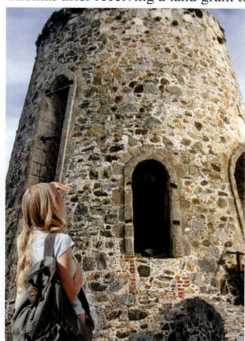

Annaberg Windmill

In 1758, a Dutchman named Salomon Zeeger,

acquired the property. Zeeger was living on St. Thomas at the time, where he met and married Anna deWindt. After their marriage, the couple moved to St. John. Following Zeeger's death, the estate went to his three daughters. Each one married a wealthy man, and the three men became joint owners of the former Constantin plantation. Under their tutelage, the plantation grew and prospered.

At some point toward the end of the eighteenth century, the sugar works was moved from Leinster Bay to its current location at Annaberg. When the relocation took place, the plantation was renamed "Annaberg" in honor of Zeeger's wife and mother of his children.

In 1796 wealthy St. Thomas merchant, James E. Murphy, purchased Annaberg. Between 1803-1807, Murphy enlarged his holdings extensively by acquiring adjoining plantations, capping off his total land interests at 1,300 acres, which included 530 acres of sugar-cane fields. Murphy also built a prominent great house at Leinster Bay. It was situated on top of a hill overlooking the surrounding waters, a point from which Murphy could proudly view his extensive holdings. Murphy died a few years after completing the house and is buried on the hilltop close to his former residence. At the time of his death, Murphy was the largest sugar plantation owner on St. John.

Following Murphy's death, Annaberg initially went to his daughter, Mary Murphy Sheen and her husband. In 1827, Catherina Sheen Murphy, a relative of James Murphy, inherited the property. Catherina was married to a wealthy man by the name of Hans Berg, who assumed title to the property by virtue of his marriage to Catherina. Hans Berg later became governor of St. Thomas and St. John. Berg continued to operate Annaberg as a sugar works until his death in 1862. After Berg's death, Annaberg and adjoining Leinster Bay were sold to Abraham C. Hill at auction. These two properties were eventually acquired by George Francis, a man who had been born enslaved on the Annaberg plantation.

George Francis' name first appears in the earliest existing census for the Annaberg property, compiled in 1835, in which he was recorded as a thirteen-year-old field laborer. Francis was a hard-working, well-respected man, who over the course of his life was able to take advantage of opportunities that would have been impossible when he was a youth. By 1860 he had gained the position of estate overseer, and two years later he received title to a 2-acre parcel of land along nearby Mary Creek, which he inherited from his former employer, Hans Berg.

When Hans Berg died, his properties were auctioned off separately. Mary Point was acquired by George Francis, and, at the same time, Abraham Hill acquired Leinster Bay and Annaberg. It was a few years later that George Francis had saved enough money to also acquire Annaberg and Leinster Bay. He purchased them from Thomas Lloyd (who had previously acquired Hill's interests in the two properties). At the time of his death in 1875, Francis had recently completed construction of a new sugar boiling house and a horsemill on the isthmus between Mary Creek and Francis Bay. It was the last facility to produce sugar on the Annaberg property.

After George Francis' death, his family found it difficult to cope with the finances of the estate, and, in 1876, Annaberg and Leinster Bay were given over by the court to St. Thomas merchant Antoine Anduze. Anduze retained an overseer on the property and converted the former Annaberg crop land to pasture. Annaberg remained in the hands of Antoine Anduze and his heirs until 1899. In that year, George Francis' son, Carl Emanuel Francis, along with his brother-in-law, Henry Clen, regained ownership of Annaberg along with Leinster Bay and Mary Point (which had also been previously lost by the Francis family).

Carl Francis and his family resided amidst the ruins of Annaberg until just prior to his death in 1936. The Francis family lived a frugal, self-sufficient existence. They grazed livestock, grew provision crops, and produced quicklime and charcoal. In 1935, Carl sold Annaberg to Herman O. Creque, and Creque's heirs eventually sold the property to the Jackson Hole Preserve in 1954, which then donated it to the park service in 1956. – **(Much of the condensed history of Annaberg detailed above is credited to extensive research completed and shared by David W. Knight Sr. in his 2002 publication, *Understanding Annaberg: A Brief History of Estate Annaberg on St. John, U.S. Virgin Islands.* We are indebted to David Knight for his valuable historical account of this major cultural landmark on St. John.)**

(See *Hiking Trails, #9 Annaberg Sugar Works, pp. 127-136,* for a complete self-guided tour and map of the ruins.)

The last stop on the tour is the Francis Bay ruins at Mary Point. There's a nice beach at Francis Bay for swimming and snorkeling. It's a good spot to end your journey with a refreshing dip and a picnic lunch. *(See #9 Francis Bay Beach, pp.164-165.)* There are good observation points along two separate paths from which to observe various species of waterfowl.

To reach the Francis Bay ruins from Annaberg, return to the intersection at the other end of Leinster Bay. Continue following the road along the water's edge to the Francis Bay Trail entrance. The trail's entrance is marked by an old warehouse, inscribed with two dates: 1814 and 1911. There is generally ample parking next to the warehouse.

Francis Bay Ruins

After parking your vehicle, follow the trail on foot. The remains of an estate house are less than 20 yards from the trail entrance.

The early history of the land here on the isthmus between Mary Creek and Francis Bay is not well documented. Much of it was once owned by officials of the Danish West India and Guinea Company. Gradually it was divided and sold off. During the nineteenth century, Hans Berg, governor of St. Thomas and St. John, was the owner of Mary Point (which included Francis Bay) and the adjoining estates of Annaberg and Leinster Bay.

After Berg passed away, other owners included George Francis and later members of the Francis family. In 1927, St. Thomas businessman, Herman Creque and his wife Emily acquired Mary Point. Eventually the property was donated by Jackson Hole Preserve to the Virgin Islands National Park.

Mary Point is also the former location of what was once the home of colorful, past-resident Ethel Walbridge McCully, who lived here for most of her life in her self-built dream house, "Island Fancy."

Ms. McCully designed the house herself and struggled for almost a decade constructing her home. It was the early 1950s; a time when workers were hard to find, and donkeys were still a main means of transporting building materials. Author Ruth Hull Low aptly depicts a flavor of Ms. McCully's irrepressible character

Francis Bay Estate House, ca 2014 (Not Ethel McCully's house).

when describing McCully's numerous celebrations and parties:

> *The party to celebrate Island Fancy's roof raising was only the first of the countless well-remembered parties Ethel McCully held there over nearly three decades…. A tiny, irrepressible, outspoken, determined 97-pound lady, Ethel was one of the gutsiest people you could ever hope to meet. Her blend of wit and perception often resulted in unorthodox behavior – sometimes startling – but always rigorously reasonable. She negotiated the sale of Island Fancy to the Department of the Interior, for the National Park, including free use, at her age of 84. As she put it to the government lawyers, "Look at the actuarial tables. I'm already dead!" At 88, for what was surely the most legendary party, she hired Caneel Bay Plantation's Sugar Mill and invited 70 friends and relatives to help her rehearse her wake, since known as "Ethel's Dry Run." It was not until 1980, at the age of 94, that she slowed down. She died in December as she was preparing to attend a Christmas party. Her actual wake, lacking her presence, was not the light-hearted occasion she planned on."* – (**St. John Backtime**, by Ruth Hull Low & Rafael Valls, p. 85.)

Ms. McCully reportedly fell instantly in love with St. John upon viewing it for the first time from the deck of an English cruise ship heading to Tortola in 1947. After the captain refused to dock and let her off, she immediately informed him that she would depart anyay. She promptly dove over the side with a bundle of belongings and swam ashore. Ms. McCully was a notoriously outspoken woman who in 1962 lobbied with a group of other local property owners to successfully strike a clause in a pending Congressional bill that would have given the Virgin Islands National Park the right to seize her beloved island home by condemnation. Ms. McCully shares the story of her island adventures in her popular book, *Grandma Raised the Roof.* She was an indestructible force; one whose favorite topic was mortality and who hated progress and any reference to her growing old.

Continuing your hike, a short distance beyond the Francis Bay Estate House, you come to a high point on the trail where you'll find a seating bench overlooking a salt pond. The salt pond attracts herons and other water birds. There are 144 or more bird species found on St. John. (See our *Checklist of Birds, pp. 179-184,* for more information.) The park service conducts ranger-guided bird hikes at Francis Bay. Check with the visitor's center in Cruz Bay for scheduling and reservations.

The beach is 0.5 miles further down the trail. It's a pleasant, stroll that takes you through dry scrub forest, circling the salt pond. You may also drive directly to the beach by returning to your vehicle and continuing to follow the road down the hill.

Pelicans are a popular attraction at Francis Bay as they plummet into the water for baitfish. Fishermen tend to follow pelicans to

Brocken Inaglory, Courtesy Wikimedia under creative commons license,
https://commons.wikimedia.org/wiki/File:Green_turtle_swimming_over_coral_reefs_in_Kona.jpg

locate the best spots for finding a good catch. Francis Bay is also a popular spot for green turtle sightings.

The green sea turtle can reach almost 40 inches in carapace length (top shell) and can weigh up to 500 pounds. It feeds on sea grasses. These turtles reach sexual maturity between 20 and 50 years. Green turtles are the largest of all the hard-shelled turtles. When laying, they produce about five nests or clutches, one every two weeks. It takes about two months for eggs to hatch. Green turtles also frequent Maho Bay and Salt Pond Bay.

End of North Shore Tour

Centerline Motor Tour to East End and South Shore
(4.0 Hours, Approx.)

The Centerline tour begins in Cruz Bay at the start of Route 10, just above the rotary near the fire station and school. Centerline is the main thoroughfare connecting Cruz Bay with Coral Bay, a tiny picturesque settlement on the east side of the island. There are no gas stations in Coral Bay, so best to fill-up in Cruz Bay before starting out. The mountainous 8-mile distance between the two points led to the creation of St. John's popular road race, "8 Tuff Miles." This annual marathon held in February attracts more than 1,500 runners, each hopeful of completing the strenuous course.

The Centerline drive offers scenic views as you twist and turn your way through the rugged hillside followed by a picturesque descent into the Coral Bay settlement. The village consists of a scattered collection of a dozen or so small businesses, including a few popular eateries where you may wish to stop and enjoy lunch.

Points of interest along the route include the remains of two former sugar plantations, Adrian (steam-powered crushing equipment still in-place) and Catherineberg (with its unique round vaulted room beneath the windmill); sites of colonial Moravian missions (Moravians played a major role in the empowerment of the enslaved population); ruins of the Danish fortress where St. John's Revolt of 1733 began; partially hidden remains of an early nineteenth-century, English battery; and a former estate house once occupied by a young Danish countess. There are also several popular beaches, including Salt Pond Beach, Little Lameshur Beach, Saltwell Bottom Beach, and Hansen Beach. (See *Beaches, East End, South Shore, pp. 166-169.)*

Getting Started
As you depart the rotary and start your drive upwards on Centerline, note changes in the vegetation, which becomes denser and

lusher as you go higher and higher. The south and east shores of St. John are considerably drier than the north shore and mountaintops; the latter receiving more than 70 inches of rainfall a year.

Less than 0.5 miles from town, you'll reach a road on the right with a sign directing you to the Bethany Moravian Church.

Bethany Moravian Church

The first Moravian missionaries, David Nitschmann and Johann Leonhard Dober, arrived on St. Thomas in 1732. While on St. Thomas they lived frugally and preached to the enslaved laborers. By 1734 they had both returned to Germany, but other Moravian missionaries continued their work, establishing churches on St.

Bethany Moravian Church

Thomas, St. Croix, and St. John as well as other islands such as Jamaica, Antigua, Barbados, and St. Kitts. Moravians were extremely pious. They came to spread their faith, but they also came with a fervent desire to improve the miserable living conditions of the enslaved population. They were highly successful at recruiting converts, and their numbers grew rapidly.

Moravians established mission stations at six locations around

St. John. The land for the Bethany mission was purchased in 1749. Launching the mission required strong faith and perseverance. Hurricanes, famines, social upheaval, and illness made it very difficult. Bethany's first full-time pastor died of fever shortly after the Bethany land was acquired, and it took five years before another resident missionary could be dispatched.

There are two historic cemeteries on the grounds of the Bethany site. The one furthest removed from the church is where the first missionaries are buried. Most of the historic buildings, including the present-day church, were damaged (primarily by storms) at various times over the years and some original features (including the church belfry) have been rebuilt or replaced.

Leaving the church, return to Centerline, and turn right. A short distance ahead you reach the Myrah Keating Clinic, the island's principal medical facility. The clinic is named after Myrah Keating, a popular nurse known for successfully employing local plant remedies in her practice. Myrah was a graduate of Tuskegee Institute and for many years was the only health-care provider on St. John. She passed away in 1994 after bringing some 500 babies into this world.

You will often find livestock (goats, cattle, and pigs) wandering, grazing, and sometimes napping in some pretty odd places on this stretch of the road. Drivers should exercise caution.

Continuing along Centerline, about 0.25 miles past the clinic, you reach a concrete bridge (a short distance beyond St. John Concrete) spanning the narrow streambed on the right side of the road. The bridge leads to the ruins of Estate Adrian, one of the oldest sugar plantations on St. John.

The area is overgrown because the park service does not have the funds necessary to stabilize the remains of all its historic ruins. Rather than clear away brush and expose ruins to rapid deterioration from the elements, vegetation is often permitted to run wild until structures can be properly stabilized. While some of the Adrian ruins are difficult to locate in the bush, the factory building is less than a 5-minute walk up the path from the road. Original steam-powered equipment is still in place.

Adrian Plantation

The Adrian plantation was established in 1718, the year Danes officially began colonizing St. John. Its first owner was Adrian Runnel. In 1725 Runnel also purchased Trunk Bay. The two plantations were merged to improve efficiency and reduce operating costs. Building and maintaining a sugar works was a costly venture as detailed in this 1768 accounting of the enterprise:

> One can form a rough estimate of the considerable expense in providing a sugar plantation with all the necessary buildings and implements. The cost of rollers alone for a sugar mill, in addition to other ironwork, comes to 500 pieces [of eight]. Since wood is expensive...the construction cost of a good windmill can run up to 9,000 pieces. A horsemill can be completely constructed for 1,000 pieces. However, on an average plantation there will be 20 mules required to power it, and each of them costs 110 to 130 pieces.
>
> The sugar cookhouse, the curing house, where sugar casks stand, [and] the still, where the rum is distilled, cannot be constructed at a cost of less than four to five thousand pieces. The purchase of sugar coppers, many of which are necessary on a large plantation, must be reckoned at over a thousand pieces of eight.
>
> Over a hundred ...[enslaved laborers] are necessary for the operation of a plantation, on St. Thomas or St. John, which is 3,000 feet long and 4,000 feet wide. With all of its buildings, sugar works, stock, and whatever pertains to all of these, the plantation is worth 50,000 to 70,000 pieces of

Adrian's Steam-Powered Equipment

eight [see below*].

On such a plantation, approximately 150,000 pounds of sugar, or 150 barrels, are produced yearly on average. From all this it can be concluded that they do quite well, making a return of ten percent, hurricanes and poor soil being taken into account.
– (C. G.A. Oldendorp, *A Caribbean Mission, 1768*, pp. 149-150, taken from an English translation by Arnold Highfield and Vladamir Barc as published in *St. John Voices*, by Ruth Hull Low, p.18.)

[* The Spanish dollar, also known as the piece of eight (Spanish: Real de a ocho), is a silver coin, of approximately 38 mm diameter, worth eight Spanish reales, that was minted in the Spanish Empire following a monetary reform in 1497. The Spanish dollar was widely used by many countries as the first international/world currency because of its uniformity in standard and milling characteristics. Some countries countersigned the Spanish dollar so it could be used as their local currency. The Spanish dollar was the coin upon which the original United States dollar was based, and it remained legal tender in the United States until the Coinage Act of 1857. Because it was widely used in Europe, the Americas, and the Far East, it became the first world currency by the late 18th century.] – Definition Courtesy *Wikipedia*, the free encyclopedia.

When you've finished looking around, return to your vehicle. A short distance beyond Adrian you come to a large sign announcing your entry into the Virgin Islands National Park. If you follow the road near the sign that leads off to the left, you arrive at the ruins of the Catherineberg windmill and adjacent factory buildings. Unlike Adrian, some of Catherineberg's ruins have been stabilized and can be safely explored.

Estate Catherineberg

The Catherineberg-Jockumsdahl plantation is one of the oldest plantations on St. John. It was a thriving sugar plantation from the eighteenth through the nineteenth centuries, after which it was eventually converted to a cattle farm. Ruins and buildings that remain from the plantation era include eighteenth-century factory buildings, windmill tower, and horsemill.

Unlike the conventional solid foundations found beneath most windmills, Catherineberg's windmill (which dates from between 1797 and 1803) sits on a round, vaulted room, which may have originally been a chapel. Working around windmills and cane-crushing rollers on sugar plantations like Catherineberg was dangerous (and often death-threatening) business, and accidents were frequent among laborers.

Many circumstances threatened the health and welfare of laborers. Often workers deliberately inflicted injury on themselves in order to purposely reduce their ability to work. They sometimes did so as a way of getting even with an especially harsh owner. Enslaved laborers knew that their owners viewed them as valuable "property." Damaging a harsh owner's "property" was seen by the victim as just retribution for abusive treatment. It was also not uncommon for workers, frustrated by their condition, to commit suicide. This was especially true among captives who had held high-ranking tribal positions in Africa.

There were not many ways for enslaved workers to escape. Some managed to run away, either alone or in small groups. Runaways were called "maroons." Maroons often tried to reach surrounding islands in search of freedom. Danish authorities made efforts to prevent their flight. For example, in 1706 an order was issued commanding that all trees near the shoreline that could be used for building canoes be cut down. Rewards were offered for capturing and returning maroons, dead or alive.

Catherineberg Windmill with Vaulted Round Room

Illness and death from tropical diseases also took a toll. The Danish government tried controlling disease by instituting a com-

CENTERLINE MOTOR TOUR/SOUTH SHORE

prehensive healthcare system to protect enslaved laborers, but after Emancipation there was little financial incentive to promote public health, and the program collapsed.

Leaving the windmill, retrace your path back to Centerline Road, and turn left. Just east of Catherineberg you pass the entrance to L'Esperance Trail. (See *Hiking Trails, #21 L'Esperance Trail, pp.142-145.*) This trail leads hikers through ruins of several early plantations. Along the way, hikers can view the island's only baobab (or "spirit") tree, which some speculate may have been carried here as a small plant (or fertilized seed) by an enslaved African. This odd-looking tree is thought by some cultures to contain the souls of the dead. It was often used as a meeting place for tribal gatherings. Some baobabs have openings at the base of their trunks that are so large the tree can be used as a place of refuge. Baobabs have been known to live more than 1,200 years.

Driving on, a short distance beyond the L'Esperance trailhead, you next reach the entrance to the Reef Bay Trail. A major highlight on this popular hiking trek includes the well-restored remains of the last operating steam-powered sugar factory on St. John. The trail also leads to some intriguing petroglyphs, whose origins have been the subject of much speculation. Informative plaques along the trail help visitors learn more about local fauna and flora. (See *Hiking Trails, #22 Reef Bay, pp. 145-157.*)

A short distance ahead, Centerline reaches its highest point before taking a sharp turn to the left and starting its steep descent down Bordeaux Mountain into Coral Bay. At its highest peak, Bordeaux Mountain rises some 1,200 feet above sea level, making it one of the tallest points on the island. Views as you descend the mountainside are wonderful. There are several convenient spots to pull over to admire the vistas and take photos.

Coral Bay

Coral Bay holds a significant place in St. John's history as the site of the island's first Danish settlement. The settlement grew steadily until the sugar economy collapsed and Coral Bay lost much of its original purpose. Eventually Cruz Bay became the island's princi-

View of Coral Bay Harbor

pal port due to its closer proximity to St. Thomas.

Look carefully toward the center of the valley as you make your descent, and you can spot the remains of a colonial windmill, now surrounded by bush. Nearby, there are also ruins of a horse-mill and sugar factory. Just to the right and in front of the windmill on a small hill is where a great house was built in the 1800s. Some speculate that this may have been the location of an earlier great house where Judge Sodtmann and his stepdaughter were killed by rebels at the start of the revolt. The windmill and surrounding ruins are accessible by road, but the structures are located on private property. They require the owner's permission to visit. One of the more intriguing sites in Coral Bay is the crumbling remains of Fortsberg, situated on the summit of the large cone-shaped hill on the east side of the harbor. This is the location where a small group of rebels attacked and overpowered unsuspecting guards in 1733, thus igniting the rebellion.

In recent years, Coral Bay has experienced a resurgence in popularity and growth. The harbor is part of a larger area known as "Hurricane Hole," a wide water body that runs far inland, offering protection to moored vessels. The steep mountains generally guard it from fierce storms, but not always, as was the case with two back-to-back 2017 hurricanes. The value of the harbor was recognized by Governor Bredal when he landed here in 1718 with his colonizing expedition. He described the harbor as "completely secure, and when you are in there, you are so confined that you only see land all the way around you."- (**Leif Calundann Larsen,** *The Danish Colonization of St. John 1718-1733*, **pp. 12-13.**) The virtues of the harbor have been repeatedly lauded over the years. Military engineer Peter Oxholm praised its attributes in a notation on his 1780 map of St. John claiming "Coral Bay is one of the best [harbors] in the West Indies...[which could, he said] hold a considerable number of warships." - **(Leif Calundann Larsen,** *The Danish Colonization of St. John 1718-1733*, **p. 14.**) Despite its many praises, Coral Bay harbor never saw the development that once seemed imminent. This was largely because sugar production on St. John never reached the level originally anticipated. There was also competition from the harbor at nearby St. Thomas. It was better located, being adjacent to a busy commercial district and consequently proved more attractive for shipping than did the remote harbor of Coral Bay.

Emmaus Moravian Church
At the heart of Coral Bay is the Emmaus Moravian Church—a large yellow structure set prominently against the hillside opposite the park. The present church was built in 1919 on the spot where a previous church was demolished by a hurricane in 1916.

The land surrounding the church was originally part of the Estate Caroline plantation owned by the Danish West India and Guinea Company. When the Company was dissolved in 1754, the land passed into private hands. In 1782 it was acquired by Governor Thomas de Malleville, who donated the property to the Moravian ministry after his conversion to the faith.

Moravians played a key role in religious instruction and education of the African population under Danish sovereignty. They began arriving in the Virgin Islands in 1732 at the urging of the sect's German founder, Count Louis von Zinzendorf, who first learned of the horrific treatment being endured by enslaved laborers while a guest at the Danish court.

Early Moravian missionaries made a conscious effort to engage the enslaved population by meeting and mingling freely among

Moravian Church, ca. 2014

them on their plantations after work hours. They also learned to speak their Creole language.

Moravians constructed schools and performed a key role in teaching the enslaved population how to read and write. When compulsory public education came into effect in the 1840s, they were asked to run the public schools at Emmaus and other locations.

Moravian missionaries were also excellent craftsmen. They were able to persuade the planters to allow them to train enslaved laborers to become artisans. As a result, many members of the Moravian congregation became skilled basket weavers, carpenters, stone masons, and coopers. These newly learned skills played an important part in ensuring the survival of the local population after Emancipation.

For the enslaved workers, attending the missions fulfilled an important need to socialize and gain self-respect, as they were not allowed to converse while working, and rarely allowed to gather amongst themselves in the evenings. By successfully completing a prescribed learning process, church members were rewarded with baptism. Some rose in the ranks of the church hierarchy and assumed various levels of responsibility.

Leaving the church, go left on Route 10. The road eventually winds its way to the extreme eastern part of St. John, a relatively remote area known simply as "East End."

East End Profile/ Basketmaking

East End is geographically defined as all land east of Haulover, which basically begins at the little concrete bridge about 0.1 miles past Estate Zootenvaal and extends east to Privateer Bay. Haulover takes its name from the fact that area residents once used nearby Haulover Bay as a launching point for their boats. The short distance at this location between the two surrounding bodies of water—Drake's Passage and the Caribbean—gave residents an opportunity to save considerable time by hauling their boats from one side to the other, rather than having to sail all the way around the east end of the island. There is a nice swimming beach at Haulover Bay on the south side of the road. *(See #12 Haulover Beach, p. 167.)*

Haulover Shoreline

Tax records dating to 1728 show the first occupied tract of land in the area was owned by John Jacob Creutzer, an employee of the Danish West Indies and Guinea Company. Creutzer used his land to grow provisions for ships. Creutzer was survived by his wife, who later married Jens Jensen. In 1747, Jensen became the governor-general of the Danish West Indies. At some point, Jensen moved to St. Croix, and the land was abandoned. This led to the arrival of a small group of Creole families from the British island of Virgin Gorda. Other relatives followed. One brought an old cotton gin, and some brought a few enslaved laborers. The community soon consisted of a core collection of closely connected families that survived on cottage industries, small-scale cotton production, provision farming, and transporting of goods by sea. Most of the residents initially settled around Hansen Bay. Later they spread out to other areas of East End. Freed persons from other nearby islands eventually added to the population.

　Before construction of Centerline Road, East End was extremely isolated and sparsely populated. As late as 1835, its inhabitants totaled only 222 persons. Following Emancipation, the population declined steadily: in 1870, 143 people lived here; in 1917, 113; and by 1938, only 78 souls resided on East End.

　Because the area is dry and arid, water was a precious and scarce resource. To be near a water source, early inhabitants lived primarily in a dozen tiny houses clustered up the hillside along the "gut" (streambed) above Hansen Bay. Water was also collected in barrels drained from rooftops. Well water was brackish and used principally for feeding livestock.

　Except for an annual boat trip to pay taxes at the Administration Building in Cruz Bay, most East End residents had little contact with the rest of St. John. Isolation fostered a keen sense of inde-

Family of basket Weaver, Lightbourne Postcard, 1906, PD –1923, Courtesy "Virgin Islands Daily News," http://www.virginislandsdailynews.com/arts_and_entertainment/basket-weaving-demonstrations-honor-st-john-tradition/article_1181169e-a85d-53c8-a7e7-b4e5723ea043.html

pendence. Members of the community worked together on projects in small "clubs" to survive and supported themselves through their trades.

Basketmaking was once an important industry on St. John. The excellent quality and beauty of St. John baskets was world renowned. Two types of baskets were produced from plants that grow here: hoop and wist. Sturdy hoop baskets were fashioned from the hoop vine *(Trichostigma octandrum)* and wist baskets from the wist reed *(Serjania polyphylla)*, a much more delicate plant. Generally, women made wist baskets and men fashioned hoop baskets. Wist baskets were used for household items such as placemats, sewing baskets, flowerpots, breadbaskets, and cup holders. Hoop baskets were used for luggage, cargo, and market baskets. Basketmaking is an extremely labor-intensive task. The process of gathering the hoop and wist was very time consuming, as was the actual process of weaving a basket. It could take anywhere from three to seven days to construct a basket. St. John baskets were originally sold from the decks of schooners on St. Croix and St. Thomas. In the 1930s they were marketed through a cooperative on St. Thomas and later to tourists who arrived on cruise ships. Many baskets made on St. John were sold at the New York World's Fair.

East End Sightseeing

East End School and Cistern

The former East End School can be seen prominently perched on a hilltop at the water's edge overlooking White Bay. It sits between two popular beaches—Saltwell Bottom Beach to the east and Hansen Beach to the west *(See #13 Hansen Beach and #14 Saltwell Beach, p. 167.)* Constructed in 1862 on private property, ownership of the school was transferred to the Moravian Church in 1913, which continued its administration even after it became a public school under U.S. ownership. The roof was blown off in 1924 and had to be replaced with assistance from the local government. In 1960 the building ceased operating as a school. For a short while, it was used as the summer house for the lieutenant governor.

A community cistern built by the Moravian Church in response to the 1903 outbreak of a typhoid epidemic is located between the school and road. The cistern was built in 1907 under the guidance and direction of Reverend Foster, pastor of the Emmaus Moravian Church at the time. The pastor's name is memorialized above the cistern door.

Carolina Corral

Located a short distance east of Skinny Legs, the corral serves as a sanctuary for local animals. Its opening in 1993 was prompted by the arrival of its first residents—two wild donkeys in need of care. Owner Dana Bartlett is passionate about the fate of these loyal, hardworking creatures. It's her self-appointed mission to keep track of all island donkeys in order to ensure their health and safety. Carolina Corral is one of several groups working to help protect and care for St. John's donkeys. From time to time, Dana's corral population includes any number of other species or "guests,"

Corral Stables

including horses, goats, dogs, and chickens. Dana is always grateful for charitable donations to help support her endeavors. Information about her enterprise can be found on her website at *http://www.horsesstjohn.com*. Visitors may want to take advantage of the corral's scenic horseback rides. They are offered twice a day, Monday-Saturday. Call 340-693-5778 or email *info@horsesstjohn.com* for more information.

St. John's Donkeys

Donkeys were originally brought to the island from Abyssinia to help with sugar-cane production. They also assisted with the manufacture of bay oil, an important industry from the 1890s to the 1940s. Workers would comb the Bordeaux mountainside picking bay leaves that were then loaded on donkeys and hauled to various stills. Eventually donkeys learned the paths to the stills. They were often set loose to complete the deliveries on their own.

CENTERLINE MOTOR TOUR/SOUTH SHORE

Some Basic Donkey Info:
• Life cycle: 45-50 years.
• 75-80 donkeys reside on St. John.
• Like to stay dry and will do anything they can to avoid getting their feet wet!
• Donkeys are natural protectors of sheep and goats, however, not fond of dogs.
• Sensitive digestive system, so it is recommended that visitors do not feed them.
...And please, don't encourage them to come to your car, as this puts them at risk of being injured by traffic.

Donkeys Grazing Along Roadside

Fort Frederiksvaern ("Fortsberg") and British Battery

The Fortsberg fortress is where the historic revolt began in 1733. Here rebels overpowered six soldiers, then signaled the start of the rebellion by firing two cannon blasts before beginning their rampage. (See *Cruz Bay Walking Tour, Franklin A. Powell, Sr. Park, pp. 44-45,* for additional narrative on the start of the rebellion.)

The insurrection lasted seven months. When it was over nearly half the plantations were destroyed.

The need for the presence of a fort was early on recognized by the Danes. The Revolt of 1733 was confirmation of that need. According to Danish historian Leif Calundann Larsen,

Jack Boucher, Courtesy Wikipedia under creative commons license, PD, https://upload. wikimedia.org/wikipedia/commons/8/85/HABS_Frederiks_Fort_St_John_USVI.jpg

CENTERLINE MOTOR TOUR/SOUTH SHORE

"the fort facilitated the colonization of St. John by reassuring apprehensive settlers that they would be protected from rebellious... [enslaved workers] as well as foreign aggressors." Despite its dual purpose, it was actually due mostly to internal concerns, that a fort was built. According to Larsen, first and foremost, it was felt that having a fort would have the psychological effect of "asserting a political authority in what was basically an undisciplined frontier society."

> *One thing both authorities and planters dreaded more than anything else, was...[an enslaved laborer] rebellion....The authorities feared it because it could easily harm production, investments, the solvency of the planters, and ultimately the revenues of the Company. Furthermore, it could be feared that the planters would ...[abandon] the island if ...[authorities] failed to create a certain feeling of security. The planters naturally feared for their lives and property.... Therefore, they needed a permanent support point and refuge in the event of serious unrest."-* The *Danish Colonization of St. John 1718-1733* by **Leif Calundann Larsen, pp. 4-11.**

The elaborate stone structure that we see at the site today is not what was in place at the time of the revolt. Rather, the current fortification was built "as an immediate consequence of the ...rebellion," says Larsen, whose research reveals instead a rather diminutive original fortification surrounded by a simple parapet "gathered together of loose stone, sand, and earth." Inside the parapet, Larsen notes, were several modest structures including a house "built of stone and brick...and a small barracks...constructed of planks covered with shingles and plants." What we see here today (and what is pictured in the 1780 drawing by Peter Oxholm) is a far more massive and sturdy structure. - **(Research, and quoted narrative taken from** *The Danish Colonization of St. John 1718-1733* by **Leif Calundann Larsen, pp. 4-11.)**

Heading east out of Coral Bay, Fortsberg can be reached by following the first dirt road on the right, just beyond Skinny Legs. The same dirt road also leads to the Carolina Corral and is marked by the corral sign at the beginning of the road. Keep following the road and go past the corral. As the dirt road turns into concrete pavement and winds further upward, watch for a deep dip. Jeeps and 4-wheel drive vehicles are best for crossing the dip. It's probably a good idea to park other cars (low-riders) just ahead of the dip and go the rest of the way on foot. After the dip, the road turns left and continues upward. A short distance ahead, you reach a "Y" in the road. (Don't turn right just yet. You will return to this point after visiting the fort.) Fortsberg is up the footpath straight ahead.

On the hillside below the fort and close to the water's edge are the remains of a former English battery. Cannons are still scattered about. To reach the battery from the fort, retrace your steps to the "Y" in the road. Turn left and follow the lower road to where it ends. *(It's a bit of a walk, if going on foot.)* Follow the short footpath the remaining distance out to the water's edge where you will find the ruins. At the time the battery was built, the Napoleonic Wars were raging in Europe. The Danes had sided with France against England, thus causing the British on Tortola to twice attack and capture St. John. The second occupation lasted seven years. The battery was built as an English stronghold to defend the invaders and ward off any attempts to recapture the island.

British Battery, Coral Bay

Privateer Bay/ Pirates

The bay is located at the very tip of the East End peninsula. Arrive at Privateer Bay by following the dirt road at the end of Route 10. Just before reaching the Privateer subdivision, you pass Hansen Bay Beach and Saltwater Bottom Beach. The beginning of the dirt road leading to Privateer Bay can be identified by a collection of mailboxes. The journey around the Privateer subdivision traverses many poorly maintained and overgrown roads, which can be difficult to navigate.

East End bays were once important boat launching spots

for residents, who relied heavily on their watercraft as a primary means of transportation. East Enders made regular runs to the market on Tortola. A typical cargo included people, livestock, vegetables, and fish. Thanks to favorable breezes, the trip to Tortola could be made on a simple "reach" and did not require time-consuming course changes. It was far easier for an East Ender to reach Tortola by boat than to get to most other places on St. John. Thus, it was not at all uncommon for a young man from East End to be dating a young lady from Tortola, rather than one from Cruz Bay.

No consideration of the history of the Virgin Islands would be complete without some reference to the years when the islands and their indented bays were the harbors and safe retreats of privateers and pirates.

Pirates and privateers were not one in the same. Piracy is defined as the simple act of robbery or criminal violence by ship or boat-borne attackers upon another ship or a coastal area, typically with the goal of stealing cargo or other valuable items. Privateering uses similar methods as piracy, but the captain acts under orders of a country authorizing the capture of merchant ships belonging to an enemy nation. This made it a legitimate form of war-like activity. Privateering was regularly employed by England and France when they were trying to gain a foothold in the West Indies. Captain Kidd was a well-known English privateer who made regular visits to the Virgin Islands.

The classic era of piracy in the Caribbean lasted from 1650 until the mid-1720s. It traces its roots to the establishment of French buccaneers in the northern part of Spanish Hispaniola. At first buccaneers were mainly hunters rather than robbers; their transition to full-time piracy was gradual and motivated in part by the efforts of Spanish authorities to drive them out of Hispaniola. Among the most infamous Caribbean pirates of the time were Edward Teach ("Blackbeard"), Calico Jack Rackham, and Bartholomew Roberts. Most early era pirates were eventually hunted down by the Royal Navy and killed or captured.

Piracy in the Caribbean declined after 1730, but even as late as 1810 a number of pirates still roamed the waters though they were not as bold or successful as their predecessors. New and faster trials denied legal representation for pirates; and this ultimately led to the execution of hundreds of these freebooters.

In the early nineteenth century, piracy in the Caribbean made a brief comeback. Jean Lafitte was one of several pirates operating in the Caribbean between the years 1820 and 1835. However, by 1846, the United States Navy had grown strong enough to eliminate the pirate threat in the West Indies, which it did.

It is a commonly held belief that pirate treasure may still be buried in and around the waters of the Virgin Islands. Nearby Norman Island is the reputed location of Robert Louis Stevenson's classic story, *Treasure Island.* Several years ago, a fortunate fisherman is said to have found a sizable collection of Spanish coins in a cave on Norman Island. It's generally believed that the fisherman's treasure may have been part of a large cargo of gold and silver stolen from the Spanish merchant ship, *Nuestra Senora de Guadalupe,* which went aground off the coast of North Carolina in 1750. The loot was apparently diverted to Norman Island where it was buried in several locations.

Picking Up the Trail

After exploring East End, return to Coral Bay. Picking up the trail at the Emmaus Moravian Church, turn left at the intersection and head south on Route 107. A few yards ahead (after passing the Pickles Deli) you reach another intersecting road leading off to the right. A brief side trip up this road takes you to the Coral Bay Organic Farm and Garden Center, owned and operated by Josephine and Hugo Roller. This 18-acre, 100% organic family farm has been providing an abundance of fresh, healthy salad greens, vegetables, and fruits to the people of St. John for more than 30 years. *Josephine's Greens* are a staple in local restaurants and are sold at Starfish Market in Cruz Bay and at the Roller's farm market at the property. Visitors are welcome.

Continuing south on Route 107, look for the Oasis Bar and Restaurant in the Coral Bay village as you start your drive along the waterfront. Behind the Oasis, local artist Greg "Paz" Myers once worked in a makeshift studio until his untimely death in August 2016.

Greg "Paz" Myers

Paz approached his artwork with passion and energy. His use of vibrant colors and bold graphic imagery makes his comic-book style of painting easily recognizable. In life, Paz was a kind and generous person. He was a minimalist who openly turned his back on materialistic trappings. Paz spent fifteen years living his eccentric lifestyle on St. John. To survive the elements, he camped out in the bush on the outskirts of Coral Bay and sometimes took shelter on abandoned boats in the harbor. Karen Granitz, former owner and founder of the Oasis, became his good friend and benefactor. Karen generously gave Paz his studio space. She also let him display and sell his artwork at her cafe.

Paz at Studio, Coral Bay

Just before reaching the Oasis you pass through a grove of red mangroves at the edge of the shoreline, identified by their tangled aerial root systems protruding above the water's surface. The plants thrive in saltwater and play a key role in maintaining St. John's ecological balance. Red mangroves populate the coastline. Black and white mangroves are found further inland. When the leaves of the red mangrove are shed, they decompose among the roots (emitting a strong smell). The process provides nourishment for small crabs and worms, which in turn are food for larger fish and birds. The drive

Paz Art

"Last Supper," Paz

along the Route 107 shoreline is scenic with panoramic views of the harbor and surrounding hillsides. Eventually the road comes to the parking area at the entrance to the Salt Pond Bay Trail, which leads to Salt Pond Bay Beach. At the far east end of the beach are two popular hiking trails—Drunk Bay Trail and the Ram Head Trail. (See also *Hiking Trails, #14 Drunk Bay* and *#15 Ram Head trails, p. 139*.)

Salt Pond Bay

Salt Pond Bay Beach is an idyllic, white-crescent stretch of sand that is popular with visitors. The beach offers a bounty of shells and broken pieces of coral to peruse. Snorkelers can enjoy exploring the shoreline and observing numerous varieties of colorful fish. *(*See *#15 Salt Pond Beach, pp. 167-168.)*

The vegetation around Salt Pond Bay Beach is largely cactus and windswept growth. The beach itself takes its name from the pond located behind the trees at the far end of the sandy stretch. It was once a primary source of salt for locals.

The pond produces salt by being sufficiently below sea level, allowing ocean water to flow naturally underground into this area, where it becomes trapped and crystallizes. In 1768, Oldendorp penned the following description of the salt-harvesting process:

CENTERLINE MOTOR TOUR/SOUTH SHORE

The salt used in these islands comes from sea water. The sea itself penetrates a good bit inland and forms a kind of pond which is called a saltpan. In these the salt crystallizes freely during the dry periods and settles to the bottom in large chunks. Additionally, a thin layer of salt forms on the surface of the water, just as if it were covered with ice. The bottom of the saltpan is a marsh and the...[enslaved laborers] stand in it up to their knees in order to remove the salt. Everyone is free to help himself to this salt, not only for his own use, but for sale as well, if he sees fit. This salt resembles saltstone though it is not white, but rather caustic. – **(C.G. A. Oldendorp,** *A Caribbean Mission,* **1768, English translation by Arnold Highfield and Valdamir Barc as published in** *St. John Voices,* **by Ruth Hull Low, p.47.)**

During colonial times, this salt pond was known widely for providing an abundance of the best salt in the area. Locals still farm the pond for personal use.

The salt pond is reached via a path accessed at the southeast end of Salt Pond Bay Beach, which connects with Drunk Bay Trail. The trail skirts the left side of the salt pond and leads out to the rugged shoreline of Drunk Bay, where creative visitors have taken to fashioning sculptures from scattered coral, shells, and wood.

For the more adventuresome hiker, there's the Ram Head Trail, which starts along the shoreline at the far end of Salt Pond Bay Beach and follows the shoreline out to Ram Head. The trail is just under a mile long and takes about 30 minutes (each way) to complete. The hike ends with a steep, rocky climb up Ram Head cliff, which juts out into the

Salt Pond

water, providing dramatic views of the seascape below. Maroons used to take refuge at Ram Head and lived off the abundance of fish that could be caught near the shore. Certain varieties of cactus supplied them with liquids and edible fruit. Runaways also benefited from the high vantage point afforded by the cliff, giving early warning of planters approaching to apprehend them.

The next and last stop on the tour is Little Lameshur Bay. If going by car (rather than on foot), the journey to Little Lameshur requires a vehicle with 4-wheel drive. The road starts about 0.5 miles beyond the entrance to the Salt Pond Beach Trail parking lot.

Little Lameshur Bay

Just beyond the dirt road leading to Great Lameshur Bay (identified by signage pointing toward the Yawzi Point Trail), you'll reach Little Lameshur Bay, an excellent beach for swimming and snorkeling. On the hillside above the beach are the ruins of a bay rum still, which can be reached by following the road a few yards beyond the beach and up the small hill. Upon reaching the rise, and looking to your left, you'll spot the ruins. Straight ahead is the entrance to the Lameshur Bay Trail and to its right is a steep uphill road *(off limits to non-official vehicles)* that leads to the Bordeaux Mountain Trail entrance. (See *Hiking Trails, #18 Bordeaux Mountain, #19 Bordeaux Peak Spur, and #20 Lameshur Bay trails, p.141.*)

A few yards beyond the entrance to the Bordeaux Mountain trailhead, the road reaches another hilltop overlooking the picturesque expanse of the

Little Lameshur Bay Beach from the Bay Factory Ruins

bay below. Here you'll find the remains of the former residence of the young Danish countess, Daisy Grevenkop-Castenskiold. Her cousin and close-childhood friend, Tanne Dinesen (Karen Blixen), was the author of *Out of Africa,* a story made popular by the 1985 American romantic movie of the same name starring Robert Redford and Meryl Streep. In the recent past, Daisy's home has been used as a park ranger residence.

In 1969-70, nearby Great Lameshur Bay was used as the Tektite I and II experimental site for manned undersea and space missions. A museum commemorating these projects was formerly located near the beach at Little Lameshur Bay. In 2017 the museum was closed due to severe hurricane damage.

Bay Rum Still and Bay Oil Business

The ruins of the bay still are largely intact. Bay leaves were once harvested on the hilltops above and carried to Lameshur where they were boiled to produce the oil.

Typically, the bay oil was then carried to St. Thomas where it was mixed with rum or alcohol and water, and then distilled by the firm marketing the product. Another method was to distill the leaves directly with alcohol, skipping the first step of conversion into bay oil. The latter method produced a far superior product. Occasionally this was done on St. John before shipment to St. Thomas. At one point, about 4,000 quarts of bay oil were being produced annually on St. John.

Story of Countess Daisy and Her Coffee Plantation
(September 11, 1888 – January 12, 1917)
Countess Daisy made two trips to St. John. The first time was in 1910 on her honeymoon with her husband, Kammerherre Henrik Grevenkop Castenskiold (Count Henrik), a notable Danish figure who had previously been Denmark's ambassador to Norway and was about to become its ambassador to Austria. They spent seventeen days in residence at the Lameshur Bay Estate House.

Henrik had earlier purchased the Lameshur Bay property along with the surrounding Reef Bay Estates of Misgunist, Hope, a portion of Parforce, Pacquereaux, and a portion of Bordeaux Estate in the Coral Bay Quarter. His holdings totaled 1,111 acres. These acquisitions came at a time when the Danish government was actively encouraging landowners like Count Henrik to recognize the investment potential of acquiring idle acreage on St. John and elsewhere in the Danish West Indies.

Daisy's second visit was in 1913, when she lived on her own at Lameshur Bay for about five months. She made a third visit to the Virgin Islands in 1916 while on a cruise to Panama and South America, but managed only a day on St. Thomas (with no stop on St. John) to survey hurricane damage.

Courtesy of Copyright Holder, Lokalhistorisk Arkir for Hammel og Favrskov

A look at Daisy's short but dramatic life engulfs us in the world of aristocracy and nobility with youthful days dominated by parties, balls, infatuations, scandals, competition riding, tennis, and golf centered around Frijsenborg Castle, Boller Castle, and the family mansion in Ny Kongengsgade, Copenhagen. Daisy was born into the count family of Krag-Juel-Vind-Frijs, where it was customary to receive royals and princes regularly. They entertained and attended social gatherings frequently. They also encouraged daughters to marry into noble families.

As the wife of an ambassador, Daisy found herself immersed in the hectic, aristocratic social life of Europe's extravagant courts in Vienna, Rome, and London. The social whirlwind suited Daisy's personality and her flirtatious nature.

Daisy's marriage to Count Henrik was likely a coupling of convenience, and perhaps aimed at annoying her father who had forbidden her to marry Count Eggert, a known womanizer with whom she partied extensively. Henrik was considerably older than Daisy and often too busy with official duties to give her much notice.

On her trips to her husband's plantation at Lameshur Bay on St. John, Daisy experienced the New World in first-class style. From the deck of her estate house at Lameshur, where she stayed with her West Indian manager, Mr. White, and his wife, Maude, she could proudly observe her husband's vast holdings. Mr. White was using the land for the production of bay leaves and lime fruits. There were also coconuts, bananas, oranges, and sweet potatoes. Mr. White was also experimenting with coffee and cacao. When coffee bushes were later found in the bush around Lameshur, the story arose that Daisy, like her childhood friend and cousin, Karen Blixen, also tried to grow coffee at Lameshur. However, during Daisy's limited five-month stay (1913-14), it is not likely there would have been enough time for such a project.

Life on St. John was far different from the excitement and gaiety of the European courts, which Daisy had enjoyed. Daisy had planned the 1913-14 visit for health and personal reasons (her self-acknowledged hope to free herself from her reliance on morphine). The five-month stay was very lonesome for Daisy. There were reports that her health deteriorated dramatically during this time. She struggled with isolation, her growing addiction to morphine, and bewildered thoughts of death as being the only way out of her situation. She was deeply concerned about the reputation of her family, especially for her father's sake, and became distraught at the thought of the disgrace her addictions would bring her family. When she returned to London in mid-April 1914, her husband thought she looked terribly weak. Nevertheless, Daisy denied it. She claimed everything went well and publicly appeared happy.

When Daisy was admitted to a hospital in Copenhagen (1914) she was diagnosed as suffering from uncontrollable consumption of morphine and excessive consumption of alcohol. The discovery prompted the conclusion that Daisy had become addicted to morphine after an operation in Copenhagen (1912). Unfortunately, subsequent recreational stays in the desert city of Biskra, Algeria and the aristocratic London life style did not help slowdown her abuse of morphine.

After six months of hospitalization in Copenhagen, they weaned her off of morphine and a placement at Romanas Sanatorium in Sweden was arranged. Here Daisy connected with the poet and artist Harriet Lowenhjelm and experienced a happy and carefree time where her life was put in sonnets and sketches. During a conversation with Harriet Lowenhjelm at the sanatorium, Daisy talked about having a boyfriend in the Caribbean. As it turned out, Daisy did not follow the Romanas cure rules and was expelled from the sanatorium. She then stayed in Stockholm for a good month, where she fell back into her old habits.

Daisy's arrival back in London (1915) was a surprise to Henrik, who knew that Daisy could not stay long in that city, as there were too many temptations for her: clothing, jewelry, drugs and thus the creation of more debt, which had become a concern for Henrik. To avoid these temptations, they took up residence on the coast along the English Channel.

In the summer of 1916, the idea arose to let Daisy sail to Panama and South America and thus be able to control and reduce her morphine abuse. Daisy was on that voyage between October-December, 1916. She returned to London at the end of 1916. On January 12th Daisy died at the age of twenty-eight. Divergent stories as to the exact circumstances of her death have emerged.

The first official statement appeared in the Danish newspapers within days of her death:

> *The Danish envoy in London, Kammerherre Henrik Grevenkop-Castenskiold has had the grief yesterday of losing his wife, Countess Anne Margrethe Krag-Juel-Vind-Frijs to Frijsenborg, daughter of County Count Mogens Frijs. Kammerherreinde Castenskiold [Daisy] had recently returned to London after a long voyage to South America with one of O.K.'s ships. Kammerherreinden [Daisy] sought healing on this trip for the predominant anemic disorder that has weakened her condition for a number of years and her condition was already at this point so critical that she took her private doctor with her on the journey. On returning home at Kirkwall, Kammerherreinden [Daisy] was apparently refreshed by the journey, but a violent flu attack followed and made such rapid progress for two days that death ensued.*

A second version of Daisy's final moments is conveyed much later by Viveka Rosencrantz, who accompanied Daisy on the 1916 voyage to Panama and South America. Viveka tells in her memoirs that Daisy took her life at the embassy by cutting her arteries with sharp razor blades.

A third version of Daisy's final moments centers on a room at the up-scale Carlton Hotel in London. Here, according to a literary account offered by author Arne Handberg Jakobsen in his 2014 historical novel *Countess Daisy,* Daisy is assumed to have died from an overdose of drugs in the presence of friends.

Daisy's Home Above Lameshur Bay

In the face of these conflicting accounts, and the absence of further validation, the exact sequence of events in Daisy's final moments seem for the moment anyway to remain somewhat of a mystery. Regardless, Daisy's story stands as a tragic tale of wealth and privilege and a spirited young woman's struggle to find peace and healing on St John. - **(Note: The brief account of Daisy's life and time on St. John is in large part credited to the research and generosity of accounts shared by Jens Ole Ravn-Nielsen, the acknowledged Danish expert on Daisy Frijs and author of a soon-to-be published book with information about her life entitled** *Kammerherreinden, A Story about Noble Ladies and Dead Libertines***.)**

Tektite Mission

Great Lameshur Bay achieved notoriety in 1969-70 when it was used by the Tektite I and II pioneering missions to observe psychological and physiological reactions that might be encountered in future manned undersea and space missions. The Tektite habitat used for these experiments was an underwater laboratory, which was the home to divers during the missions. The habitat appeared as a pair of silos - two white metal cylinders 4 m in diameter, 6 m high, joined by a flexible tunnel and seated on a rectangular base.

On February 15, 1969, four U.S. Department of Interior scientists (Ed Clifton, Conrad Mahnken, Richard Waller and John Van Derwalker) descended to the ocean floor to begin the first diving mission dubbed "Tektite I." By March 18, 1969, the four aquanauts had established a new world's record for saturated diving by a single team. On April 15, 1969, the aquanaut team returned to the surface with over 58 days of marine scientific studies. Much of the research for Tektite I centered on humans in this new environment. Topics investigated included biology (blood changes, sleep patterns, oxygen toxicity, decompression and decompression sickness, microbiology, and mycology). Tektite II, expanded its focus to include ecology.

Tektite II was carried out in the summer of 1970. It comprised multiple missions lasting 10–20 days with four scientists and an engineer on each mission. The fifth mission, designated Mission 6-50, was an all-female saturation dive team. The Tektite II missions were the first to undertake in-depth ecological studies from a saturation habitat. When Tektite II ended the habitat was placed in storage in Philadelphia.

Tektite III evolved when a group of interested parties purchased the habitat from for $1.00 with the stipulation it would be removed from its storage facility. The habitat was trucked across the United States to Fort Mason in San Francisco where it was placed on display. Attempts were made to refurbish the habitat so it could be used in San Francisco Bay as a teaching tool, but unfortunately, lack of funds ended the project and the habitat was moved to storage along the Oakland Estuary in 1984. After several years, the habitat deteriorated. In 1991, it was dismantled by welding school students and the metal was recycled.

Underwater Habitat

End of Centerline and South Shore Tour

Hiking Trails

Listed here are twenty-three hiking trails that help connect visitors with the beautiful beaches, bays, mountains, and historic past of St. John. Many trail entrances are identified by signs that indicate their level of climbing difficulty. Most are well maintained, but some occasionally become difficult to traverse due to rapid growth of vegetation. The park service does some of the work, but most trail maintenance is done by volunteers. Three trails—Annaberg, Cinnamon Bay Loop, and Reef Bay—have park service plaques describing vegetation and historical points of interest. Much of the original information on these plaques has been duplicated in this guidebook. As a further aid, there are descriptive checklists at the back of the book picturing popular fauna and flora, which you are likely to encounter while hiking.

Our list of trail hikes is meant to serve as a useful guide to the most popular hiking paths. Some trails that once accessed early plantations have been concealed by the bush and remain out of reach to the average hiker. Park rangers at the visitor center can provide further guidance on hiking trails and their level of difficulty and accessibility.

Our trail guide is divided below into three sections—North Shore, Centerline, and South Shore. *(Trails shown on the centerfold map display numbers in "green" that correspond to the numbers next to the trail descriptions listed below. Included also is a separate map showing the Cruz Bay area network of trails.)* Ranger-led hikes are available for two trails, L'Esperance (typically November–April) and the Reef Bay Trail (generally year-round). Woodland trails can often be steep, uneven, rocky, and slippery in places. You'll need sturdy, closed-toe shoes, and a sure foot. Take plenty of water, some snacks, a lunch, and a hat. Mosquito repellent is a good idea. Some of the trails offer a chance for a refreshing swim at beaches along the way. The two ranger-led hikes end with an optional 40-minute boat ride back to the Cruz Bay visitor center.

For more information visit the NPS website at *https://www.nps.*

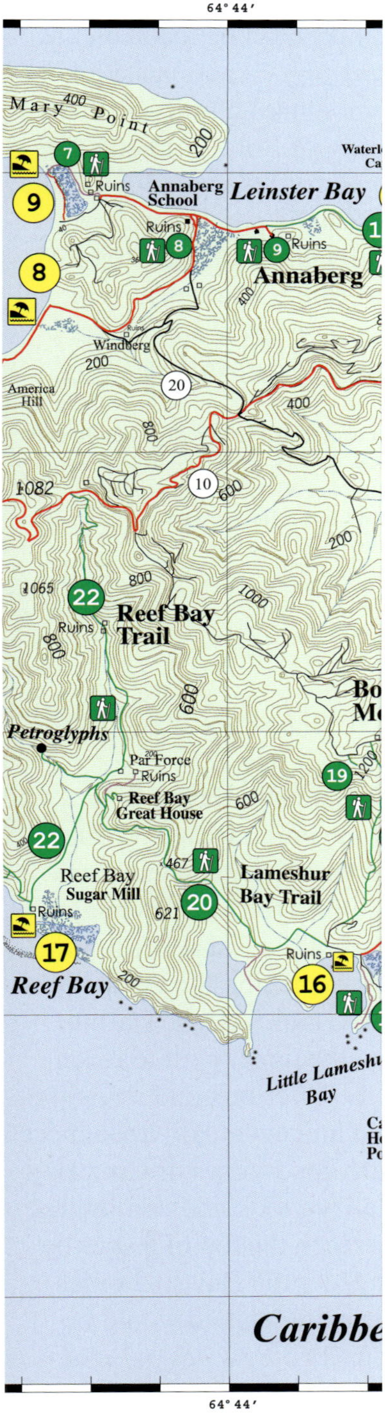

64° 44′

Mary Point 400
200
Waterl
Ca
Ruins
Annaberg School
Leinster Bay
9
Ruins
8
9 Ruins
Annaberg
8
Windberg 200
America Hill
20
400
800
1082
10 600
200
1065
22
800
Ruins
Reef Bay Trail
1000
800
600
Bo
M
Petroglyphs
Par Force 200
Ruins
19
Reef Bay Great House
600
22
.467
Lameshur Bay Trail
Reef Bay Sugar Mill
20
621
Ruins
200
Ruins
17
16
Reef Bay
Little Lameshu Bay
Ca
He
Po

Caribbe

64° 44′

St. John Map

STJ ON FOOT AND BY CAR

gov/viis. Reservations for the ranger-led hikes can be made on the Friends website at *https://www.friendsvinp.org*. Experienced hikers looking to explore some of the less common hiking trails on their own may want to order or download a copy of Bob Garrison's *The Last Trail Bandit Guide to the Hiking Trails of St. John* (2014). The map is printed in a 20" x 34" format and can be purchased directly from Bob for $3.00. Send payment to Bob Garrison, P.O. Box 394, Henniker, NH 03242. You can also email Bob with questions or requests at *rgarrison@mcttelecom.com* or *bob@trailbandit.org*. Bob's map can be downloaded free at *http://www.trailbandit.org.*

Note: Information related to our trail descriptions is credited to research conducted by Bob Garrison that is shared in his *Last Trail Bandit Guide to Hiking Trails of St John (2014)* and to information compiled and published by the NPS. We are especially grateful to Bob Garrison for providing the source material for our centerfold map and our map of the Cruz Bay area network of trails.

North Shore

(1) Lind Point Trail (1.1 miles, 1 hour)
Difficulty: Moderately Strenuous

Connects the National Park Visitor Center at Cruz Bay with the Battery Overlook, Salomon Bay, and Honeymoon Beach. Primary access is via the stairway located behind the visitor center. There is a second point of access (upper Lind Point Trail), which begins on North Shore Road across from the start of the Caneel Hill Spur Trail *(Number #3 below)*. From the stairway behind the visitor center, it is a half-mile hike to the Battery Overlook. As you start up the trail, you quickly reach a "Y." Follow the upper path to reach the Overlook; the lower route bypasses the Overlook and skirts the hillside below. The two paths form a loop and eventually reconnect at two separate points up ahead. There are good views of Cruz Bay harbor from the Overlook. Departing the Overlook and continuing on for another 0.7 miles, you eventually reach the top of a spur on your left that leads downward to remote Salomon Bay (0.2 miles). There is a beach at Salomon Bay, but the better choice would be Honeymoon Beach a bit further up ahead. (See *Beaches, #1 Honeymoon Beach, pp. 159-160.)*

HIKING TRAILS 117

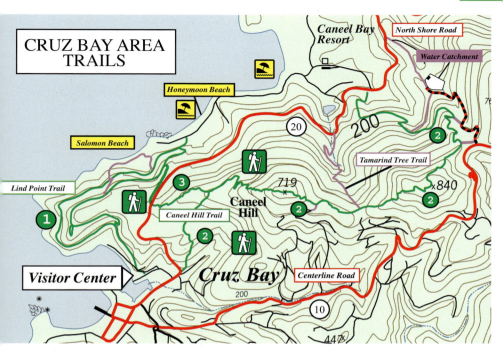

Before reaching Honeymoon Beach, you'll pass the interconnecting upper Lind Point Trail, which heads upward and connects with North Shore Road.

(2) Caneel Hill Trail (2.4 miles, 2 hours)
Difficulty: Strenuous

Starting just north of Mongoose Junction on North Shore Road, this trail joins Cruz Bay village with North Shore Road near the entrance to Caneel Bay Resort. A 0.8-miles climb from Cruz Bay leads to a scenic overlook atop Caneel Hill (elev. 719 feet). At the low point of the saddle between Caneel Hill and Margaret Hill, the Tamarind Tree Trail enters on the left. This pleasant but seldom used trail crosses a gut near the bottom, which is rocky and can be slippery when wet. Past the Tamarind Tree Trail junction, the Caneel Hill Trail winds its way up Margaret Hill (elev. 840 feet) and eventually descends to North Shore Road. Before reaching North Shore Road, you pass three side trails on the right, intersecting the Caneel Hill Trail at separate points. All three trails take you to the Water Catchment Trail, which leads to a large water basin built in

1955 to supply water to Caneel Bay Resort guests.

(Coming from the other direction, the Water Catchment Trail starts at North Shore Road near the entrance to Caneel Bay Resort. It ascends the hill by following a road as far as the water catchment. At the water catchment it turns into an old roadbed and continues up to Centerline Road, passing the three side trails that connect with the Caneel Hill Trail.)

(3) Caneel Hill Spur Trail (0.8 miles, 40 minutes)
Difficulty: Moderate

Starts where it connects with the upper Lind Point Trail at North Shore Road (Route 20) at a point overlooking Cruz Bay and Caneel Bay and continues up to join the Caneel Hill Trail.

(4) Peace Hill Trail (0.1 miles, 10 minutes)
Difficulty: Easy

Trail leads from the parking lot to a scenic, grassy overlook where you'll find the ruins of a sugar works and windmill 2.8 miles from Cruz Bay just off the North Shore Road. Enjoy extensive views of the Atlantic and St. John's northern shoreline.

(5) Cinnamon Bay Loop Trail (0.5 miles, 30 minutes)
NPS, Self-Guided Trail
Difficulty: Easy

The loop trail is located on the south side of the road just east of the entrance to the Cinnamon Bay Campground. On the hike, you'll visit the ruins of an old sugar factory and bay rum still and learn about flora and fauna and some old-time local ways. You can also view the ruins of a great house and a small Danish cemetery. The first part of the trail consists of raised wooden walkways that wind through most of the factory ruins. The walkways are handicap-accessible and accommodate wheelchairs. Next comes the beginning of the woodland loop trail. NPS descriptive plaques are located along the entire trail route and are capitalized (for reference) in bold-faced type in this text. Information from the plaques is included in this guidebook.

View Across Horsemill

The first plaque at the start of the trail shows your location and the **TRAIL ROUTE** you will be following.

Walking up the trail towards the sugar factory, note the circular platform to the left. The **HORSEMILL** is where cane stalks were crushed between iron rollers to extract the juice. Power to rotate the rollers was supplied by horses, mules, or oxen harnessed to a central shaft and forced to walk in circles. The cane juice extracted from the stalks was funneled by gravity into the **SUGAR FACTORY** where it was heated and boiled in a series of pots. Beds where the pots were seated are still visible. The spent cane stalks were stacked in a shed where they would dry to be used later as fuel to feed the fires under the boiling kettles. Take a moment to walk through the boiling room where you will observe the remains of these cauldrons. After exploring the sugar factory, return to the plaque in front of the factory and follow the trail along the right-hand side of the building.

The large circular chimney adjacent to the factory is attached to ovens where bread was baked to feed workers. Next look for the plaque describing the **TYRE PALM**, the only remaining palm native to St. John. The plant's broad leaves were used as thatching for pre-Columbian and colonial huts and for making durable brooms, used even in modern times. The plant's fibrous inner bark could also be woven into hammocks and fish traps.

A few steps beyond the factory, the trail winds to the right and leads to the remains of a bay rum still; identified by its pyramidal chimney. Just to the right of the bay still, a marker points to the entrance of the loop trail. Before starting the woodland path, you may want to first take a short detour by walking across the small stone bridge, which leads to the remnants of the **CINNAMON BAY ESTATE HOUSE** and several outbuildings. If you prefer to wait, you also have a chance to view these structures later in the hike when the loop trail circles back around by them at the end of the route.

In the 1700s and early 1800s, a modest wood and masonry structure at this location served as the home for the Cinnamon Bay Estate owners and managers. It was last occupied in 1968. A baking oven is located to the right (east side) of the house. There were only a few "great houses" on St. John, and most were not lavish dwellings. Many estates employed overseers with owners residing on St. Thomas or abroad. The plaque shows an artist's rendering of a typical estate house. Much of the house has been damaged and removed over time, but the original stairway leading up to the main floor is still visible.

Note the **CALABASH (GOBI)** plaque. The tree produces hard, smooth-walled gourds up to 12 inches in diameter. Calabashes have been used for years by St. John inhabitants to produce cups, bowls, bird feeders, and musical instruments. The shape of the calabash can be manipulated by tying strings around it, or otherwise binding it, while it is growing. A local expression of annoyance, "I'll knot your head," may come from this shaping technique.

Retrace your steps back across the stone bridge, turn right at the bay rum still, and head up the path. The surrounding hillsides are dotted with **BAY RUM TREES**, easily identified by their smooth brown trunks. These trees thrive in the rich soil and damp climate found on this side of the island. At one time, children used to climb the trees to pick the leaves and drop them to women waiting below with baskets. The precious bay oil was extracted and combined with rum and other alcohols to make a scented perfume. If you crumple a leaf between your fingers, you'll immediately experience its intoxicating rich aroma. The chimney and cooling system behind you were part of the still where leaves were steamed to remove the oil.

In St. Thomas this oil was combined with other additives to make St. John Bay Rum, a popular after-shave and toilet water in the late 1800s and early 1900s.

The only mammals considered to be **NATIVE ANIMALS** are six species of bats. They are a major source of pollination and mosquito control. Watch and listen for them at dusk.

Mongooses and donkeys seen along the trail were introduced here by plantation owners. Green iguanas, also seen here, may have been introduced by St. John's earliest settlers, pre-Columbian South Americans, who began arriving around 770 B.C. Other lizards, along with some insects and amphibians, likely "rafted" to St. John on floating logs and debris or came overland during the last ice age when sea levels were much lower.

About 150 yards past the bay rum still you come to a colonial **DANISH CEMETERY**. Plantation residents were often buried in above-ground crypts. The size of a gravestone

Family Burial Site

indicated the economic status of the person buried there. Enslaved laborers were usually buried in unmarked graves along beaches or on estate land where they had worked. On occasion, enslaved laborers, as well as freed people of color and employees, were also buried alongside or nearby the plantation owner and family members. The largest monument in this cemetery belongs to Anna Margarethe Berner Hjardemaal, the wife of Nicolai Severin Hjardemaal, who purchased the 300-acre plantation in 1834. Anna died at the age of 51, only two years after the purchase. The couple had five children, but it is uncertain how many resided here at Cinnamon Bay. The family lived in a plantation house on nearby America Hill. The land at Cinnamon Bay was used for sugar cane and other crop cultivation. Seventy-eight enslaved laborers lived on the plantation.

Leaving the cemetery, turn left. Continue walking up the trail. The next plaque describes some of the **BIRDS OF THE FOREST** that you are likely to spot along the trail. Permanent avian residents include smooth-billed anis, zenaida doves, and pearly-eyed thrashers *(pictured on the plaque)*. As forests Caribbean-wide continue to disappear due to development, protected ones such as this become increasingly valuable as winter habitats for many North American migratory birds such as the hooded warbler, the American redstart, and over twenty species of songbirds that take refuge here each season.

The next plaque discusses **TERRITORIALITY.** Watch closely on walls and tree trunks for indigenous anole lizards (male crested anolie, pictured on the plaque) that display a reddish throat pouch, or dewlap, to show territoriality. This combined with push-ups, warns off competing males, attracts females, and protects feeding grounds. Known locally as "tree lizards," anoles are not true chameleons, despite their ability to change their skin color for camouflage.

The dark, round masses up in trees *(pictured on the next plaque)* are termite nests. These **NATURAL RECYCLERS** are blind insects that access dead wood on the ground and elsewhere by tunnels thru which they follow one another's scents. The fallen, abandoned nests and tunnels are rich in nitrogen (a natural fertilizer) and are recycled into the forest floor. The activity of termites, wood borers, and beetles, as well as the decomposition of various fungi, helps build and enrich the soil at an accelerated rate.

If you look closely you may spot faint lines of fallen **TERRACE WALLS** on the hill above. The steep terrain could only be utilized for cultivation of sugar cane by first leveling sections of land behind low stone walls. Rain would soak into the ground more rapidly with this system as well. Seen pictured here is a terraced slope with workers cutting cane and carrying bundles of cane stalks. Most of the back-breaking toil of clearing virgin forests, constructing the walls, and cultivating sugar cane was accomplished by people whose destiny was decided for them – captive laborers imported from West Africa.

A few yards ahead, the path dips down and crosses a **DRAINAGE GUT** (or natural streambed). Historically, many of the larger guts probably had trickling water much of the year. Scientists believe that when the forests were cut down the loss of absorbent soil and humus caused the entire water table to drop. During heavy rains these guts become raging torrents. In some guts, spring-fed pools provide drinking water for animals even in severe droughts.

The huge trees with the large green leaves growing along the edge of the gut are **MAMMEE APPLES**, a brown fruit used to make jams and preserves. Often planted for shade, this Caribbean tree bears its large round fruit throughout the year. These as well

Mammee Apple, Fibonacci CC BY-SA 3.0, Courtesy Wikimedia under GNU free documentation license, https://commons.wikimedia.org/w/index.php?curid=575161

as other native and introduced fruit trees, commonly found in wet ravines, are some of the largest trees on the island. Smaller, slower-growing trees found in the dry forest may actually be older despite their inferior size. Since tropical trees do not produce annual growth rings, their ages are usually estimated.

After crossing the gut, you come to a plaque identifying a **CACAO TREE**. The cacao, or chocolate tree, has become one of the best-known economic plants with New World origins. Protruding from the trunk and branches of this Mexican native are brown pods (pictured on the plaque) that contain bitter seeds, which are ground and roasted to prepare chocolate. In the early 1900s cacao was one of many crops grown on the Cinnamon Bay plantation.

A little further on you'll come to a plaque depicting a **MILLIPEDE**. "I remember when I first saw a millipede and ran to show it off," recalls one St. Johnian. The local response I received was, "It will pee in yoh eye and blind yoh!" The "gongolo," as it's locally called, is a black, shiny millipede often found on the bark of trees and shrubs. It secretes an iodine-like substance that can cause temporary blindness or severe burning of the skin. However, the same fluid is used as a remedy for toothaches and cuts.

The next plaque identifies a **MANGO TREE.** This native of India, flowers in winter and spring. Fruits mature between March and October. The pulp is eaten raw or made into preserves. Some people may experience an allergic reaction to the flower or skin, since the mango is distantly related to poison ivy and other well-known allergy-producing plants. A tidy way to eat the fruit is to stand in the sea, as a sweet ripe mango is very juicy. The ground-up pit of the fruit was said to control intestinal parasites in humans.

A common critter found along the trail is the **GOLDEN ORB SPIDER**. The golden orb *(pictured on the next page)* is a nonpoisonous spider that spends a great deal of energy spinning webs in trees and across paths. This harmless member of the orb-weaving family is noted for its strong webs in which the much larger female is usually seen in the center. The web is made of a silky, liquid-like substance and is so strong that it was used to make sewing thread years ago. If one strand of this intricately woven web is

Mang Chris.urs-o Maria Marinho, Courtesy Wikimedia under GNU free documentation and creative commons licenses, https://commons.wikimedia.org/wiki/File:Mangifera_indica._Tropical_Brazil.JPG

broken, the web becomes unbalanced.

Another plaque identifies the location of a former **CHARCOAL PIT**. Charcoal was important to early locals who used it as a heat source for cooking meals in coal pot ovens. It was manufactured by stacking select hardwood saplings and other vegetation in a mound, covering them with earth, and then lighting the mound on fire. The wood smoldered and became charcoal. Charcoal making was hard work. This arduous task is described in detail below by Ethel Best in a 1936 U.S. Department of Labor report:

> Men and woman work together in the charcoal industry. The men cut down the trees and dig the pit and pack it. The fire smolders from 24 hours to 48 hours; then men and women rake out the hot charcoal, and after it has cooled, they pack it in sacks or cans and barrels for shipping. The price varies according to the supply and demand. Usually a barrel brings from 30 to 50 cents, but occasionally the price rises to 80 cents. A pit may contain anywhere from 10 to 40 barrels, and as it takes two or three weeks to cut and collect the wood, the product of a month's work would be less than two pits a month. The work is very heavy, dirty, and, when the coal is hauled out, very hot. - **(Ethel Best, *Woman's Bureau Bulletin* No. 142, 1936 U.S. Department of Labor Report, published in Ruth Hull Low's *St. John Voices*, p. 37.)**

Ashwin06k, Courtesy Wikimedia under creative commons license, https://commons.wikimedia.org/wiki/File:Giant_Golden_Orb_Weaver_(Ventral_Side).jpg

SWEET LIME is described on the plaque near the end of the trail. Despite its name, this citrus fruit from India tastes a little bitter when eaten. The bigger and older the limes get, the sweeter they taste. Sweet lime has become aggressively invasive on the island, forming impenetrable thickets in many of the more recently disturbed moist forests. When in bloom, the white flowers smell like orange blossoms. Sweet limes can be cooked, and the liquid extracted and mixed with sugar to produce a refreshing beverage or food additive. The sticky fruit was once used as a glue substitute. A few feet further, and you emerge at the ruins of the Cinnamon Bay Estate House where the trail ends.

(6) Cinnamon Bay Trail (1.1 miles, 1 hour)
Difficulty: Strenuous

This forested trail, beginning 300 feet east of the entrance to Cinnamon Bay Campground, follows an old Danish road up, steeply at first, to Centerline Road, with a view of Cinnamon Bay along the way. At 0.12 miles, a side trail on the left, leads up 0.38 miles to a ruin on America Hill with great views of Maho Bay.

(7) Francis Bay Trail (0.5 miles, 20 minutes to the beach) Difficulty: Moderate

To reach the trail, if coming from the direction of Annaberg, continue following the road along the edge of the water at Mary Creek. The entrance to the trail is adjacent to an old warehouse at the far western end of Mary Creek, inscribed with two dates: 1814 and 1911. There is a parking lot next to the warehouse. A few yards down the trail takes you to the ruins of the Francis Bay Estate House. Just after the estate house there is a bench where you can sit and look out over the salt pond and observe various water birds. *(The park service conducts bird watching hikes at Francis Bay. Inquire at the visitor center in Cruz Bay for more information.)* Across the trail from the bench there is a vague side trail that leads up behind the estate house to several much older ruins. The main trail winds down the hill, terminating at the beach at Francis Bay. (See *Beaches, #9 Francis Bay Beach, pp. 164-165.*)

(8) Annaberg School Trail (0.2 miles, 15 minutes)
Difficulty: Moderate

This trail leads to ruins of one of the Caribbean's oldest public schools. From the school, enjoy fine views of Mary Point, Leinster Bay, and Tortola. Caution: Pay attention to road traffic when entering and exiting the trail.

(9) Annaberg Sugar Works (0.2 miles, 30 minutes)
NPS, Self-Guided Trail
Difficulty: Easy

The ruins of the Annaberg sugar works are at the end of the paved Leinster Bay Road on the north side of St. John. The historic trail is only about 0.2 miles and takes roughly 30 minutes to complete. It brings you through the ruins of what was once St. John's most prosperous sugar factory, where you will learn how each of the components described below served in the production of the island's key colonial exports of raw cane sugar, molasses, and rum. The park service has stabilized much of the Annaberg sugar works to preserve it from further deterioration. STAY ON THE TRAIL, and DO NOT CLIMB ON THE RUINS. **Some of the ruins suffered extensive damage from the 2017 hurricanes. Visitors are asked to refrain from entering areas where signage prohibits access.** If the trail along the east side of the building is impassable at the time of your visit, the lower level of the sugar factory, rum still, and firing tunnels can be reached by following the path around the west side of the complex. Refer to the map provided on the next page to aid with identifications. The alphabetization on the map (A, B, C, etc.) corresponds to the alphabetization of descriptions that follow. There are also some park service plaques along the route to help identify key components of the sugar works. The trail begins a few steps up the hill from the circular paved driveway. Follow the path that leads off to the left.

(A) Village - On the slope below the wall, the remains of twenty-one or more enslaved laborer cabins have been identified. Sugar production throughout the West Indies relied almost exclusively on enslaved labor, and Annaberg was no exception. Planting, harvesting, and processing sugar cane required a tremendous amount of

128 STJ ON FOOT AND BY CAR

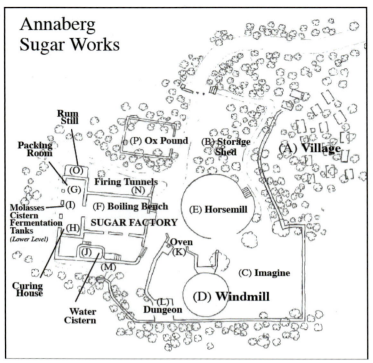

Adaptation of a Map Appearing in Doris Jadan, "A Guide to the Natural History of the St. John"

hard work. Unfortunately, it was enslaved labor that made sugar production profitable, and during the seventeenth and eighteenth centuries the African trade carrying captives to the West Indies developed hand-in-hand with the rise of the Caribbean sugar industry.

With a lime concrete floor and a door at one end, each enslaved laborer's cabin housed a family or served as bachelor quarters. Posts were set in masonry walls made from branches woven to form "wattle" that was daubed with a lime and mud mixture. Roofs were thatched with palm leaves. Women did some of their cooking at a small oven

Enslaved Laborer Cabin, Artist Unknown, Courtesy NPS, PD

within the village. Laborers grew their own fruit and vegetables on part of the village land. Some sold excess food and occasionally some saved enough money to buy their freedom.

(B) Bagasse House - The crushed stock of sugar cane, called "bagasse" or "magass," was dried and stored in sheds to be used as fuel. These stone columns are all that remain of the shed at Annaberg.

(C) Imagine - All the slopes above you were once covered with cane. With a short-handled knife, called a "cane bill," laborers cut the cane, stripped the leaves, and tied stalks into bundles. Then, loading the bundles on a mule or cart, they hauled the cane to the Annaberg factory where the juice was extracted by a crushing process. Sugar cane was often slid down the hillside on wooden skids, a process known as "shooting sugar." Before sugar cane could be planted, the rocky slopes were terraced, and the soil was turned and fertilized. Sugar cane could be planted at any time of the year provided the soil was sufficiently damp. The longer the plant grows, the more sugar it bears. The stalks grew quickly. On colonial Danish plantations, harvesting usually began around the

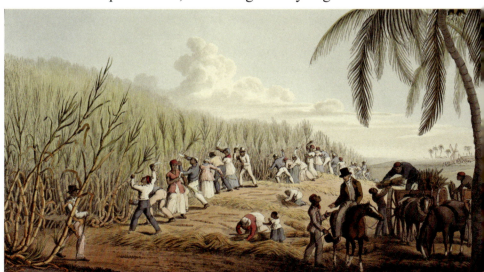

William Clark, British Library Collection, originally published 1823, Courtesy Wikimedia, PD, https://commons.wikimedia.org/wiki/File:Slaves_cutting_the_sugar_cane_-_Ten_Views_in_the_Island_of_Antigua_(1823),_plate_IV_-_BL.jpg

first of the year and lasted about six months. A 1768 narrative by C.A. Oldendorp provides a detailed account of the process:

> *In the Danish islands, sugar cane grows to the height of a man.... The cane stalk is approximately one inch in thickness.... The stalks consist of various segments, from whose joints protrude 'eyes,' or small buds, which essentially represent an equivalent number of new plants. In fact, the new plants grow out of the 'eyes' when they are placed in the earth. Under the thin wood-like skin of the cane is contained a white pulp, from which the sugar juice is produced.*
>
> *The sugar cane requires a period of 15 or 18 months to attain its complete maturity. The degree of soil quality makes a significant difference. Once a field has been planted, six, ten, or more harvests can be taken from it without necessity of replanting. This is because the old roots repeatedly push forth new stalks or new plants, which are called ratoons.... According to the testimony of elderly residents, a cane field in the Princess section of St. Croix had produced ratoons for 24 years in succession.*
>
> *Sugar cane is planted in the same manner as the grapevine. Holes of equal size are dug in regular intervals in rows as straight as a die.... The Holes are spaced a foot and a half apart; a space of three feet is left between the rows.... When a field is replanted the holes are dug in the area between the rows, as in fallow soil. Two or three pieces of mature sugar cane cut into segments approximately a yard long are placed horizontally in a hole in such a way that the knobs, or 'eyes,' on the sides come to lie alongside one another.* – **(C.G. A. Oldendorp.** *A Caribbean Mission, 1768,* **English translation by Arnold Highfield and Valdamir Barac as published in** *St. John Voices,* **by Ruth Hull Low, p. 17.)**

(D) Windmill - If a steady wind blew, the cane was brought to the windmill to be crushed. Revolving "sails" turned a central shaft that rotated a set of three large rollers, crushing the stalks. The juice then ran down the rollers into a receiving tank where it was held until the factory was ready to process it. When ready, a gate was opened, and the juice passed into a lead-lined, wooden gutter and flowed by gravity into a tank or "clarifier" in the boiling house (or room) in the factory building south of the horsemill.

A wooden turret at the top of the windmill tower could be rotated to point the sails into, or away from, the wind to engage or disengage the machinery. The turret was controlled by a long wooden pole. A small built-in fireplace inside the windmill provided light and warmth. It may also have been used to heat water for washing the rollers. The Annaberg windmill was among the largest on St. John. It is 34 feet in diameter at the base, 20 feet at the top, and 38 feet high. Windmills were not unusual in the Virgin Islands. Some 140 windmills once operated on St. Croix, which was the most successful of the U.S. Virgin Islands in terms of sugar production. St. John had only five windmills, and their period of operation was relatively short.

Windmill Diagram, Artist Unknown, Courtesy NPS, PD

(E) Horsemill - The wind was not always dependable. In calm weather cane stalks were crushed on this circular horsemill. Here mules, oxen, or horses (occasionally) were harnessed to poles and plodded around the circular course, turning three upright iron rollers in the center of the platform. Just like with the windmill, laborers passed the cane between the rollers, which crushed the stalks and released the juice, which flowed into the factory's clarifier tank. Today, none of the actual machinery that made up the horsemill or the windmill remains at Annaberg. The small cook shed that now stands on the horsemill platform was built long after the factory ceased operation.

(F) Boiling House and Bench - On the west side of the upper level of the factory building is the raised boiling bench, which originally held two "batteries" of four round-bottomed kettles each, referred to as "coppers." The clarifier tank stood at the center of the boiling bench. Sometime in the 1800s, the boiling bench at Annaberg was downsized to a single set of four coppers where the heated cane juice was ladled into successively smaller and hotter coppers, evaporating more and more moisture from the cane juice. Cane juice from the mills entered the boiling house through the square hole in the wall directly above the north end of the boiling bench. Two separate fires fed with dried cane stalks ("bagasse") in furnaces outside the wall below, heated the two rows of coppers from beneath. Damper doors located in a row beside the fire doors controlled the heat directed at the coppers above. Enslaved laborers, and later paid workers, ladled the juice from one copper to the next. During the boiling process, lime powder or ash was added to the juice to help separate impurities by floating them to the top. Workers skimmed off these impurities, which were collected and used in the rum making process or fed to the estate's animals. From the last and smallest copper, they poured the concentrated and purified sugary liquid into flat, wooden, lead-lined pans located along the wall of the east side of the boiling house to cool and crystallize into muscovado. Knowing when to remove the condensed juice from the last copper was the job of expert "sugar cookers," who were among the most valued of the workers on a plantation. If the juice was left in the copper too long it would burn, but if it was removed too early it would not crystallize upon cooling. During the cooling process, the sugar was raked to avoid clumping and ensure that uniform crystals formed.

Pi3.124, Courtesy Wikipedia under creative commons license, https://upload.wikimedia.org/wikipedia/commons/a/a8/Annaberg_Plantation_boiling_room.jpg

In order to visualize the location and inter-relationship of the boiling house, packing room, curing house, molasses cistern, and fermentation area in the Annaberg factory building, it is helpful to note that the building on the south side of the boiling bench "F" was once a *three-story structure*. The *ground floor*, "I," housed the molasses cistern and fermentation tanks. The *second floor* contained the curing house "H" and the packing room "G". These two rooms were on the same level as the boiling bench "F." The *third floor* (no longer there) is where the manager or overseer had lodgings.

(G) Packing Room - On the *second floor* (level with the boiling bench in the boiling house) were *two rooms*: the first room was the packing room (located directly behind the boiling bench, on the west side of the building). The packing room was used to pack the cool, crystallized sugar (which was removed from the cooling trays) into barrels ("hogsheads").

(H) Curing Room - After packing the hogsheads with crystallized sugar, the barrels were rolled into an adjoining curing room (located on the east side of the same floor), which had a grated floor with channels that carried drippings from the hogsheads to a molasses cistern ("I") on the *ground floor* directly below. After the hogsheads had completely cured (3 to 4 weeks), they were sealed, loaded on ships, and sent to markets overseas. Each hogshead weighed about 1,600 pounds.

(I) Molasses Cistern and Fermentation Tanks ("Butts") - Some of the drippings that fell into the molasses cistern on the *ground floor* were drawn off and packed into barrels as molasses. The rest were transported into the "still house," located on the west side of the *ground floor*. On the floor of the still house were two fermentation tanks (known as "butts") supported by wooden trestles. The butts were filled with water, molasses, and other sugar-rich by-products collected at each step of the sugar-making process. The fermented liquid mixture was called "mash." The butts held the fermented liquid used in the still located outside the factory to produce rum (See "O" below.)

(J) Water Cistern - Located in the room situated on the far east side of the factory opposite the boiling house and bench you will see two sets of stairs. One set gave access to the water cistern, while the other led up to the (now removed) third-floor living area. Through the opening next to these stairs you can look down onto the ground floor where the molasses cistern and fermentation tanks ("I") were located. A large quantity of water was needed to produce sugar and to support the people living and working on the estate. As ground water was not readily available, rainwater from the roof flowed through gutters into this cistern. The cistern holds about 20,000 gallons. Water used in the factory was also collected and stored on the hill above and transported to the factory by an aqueduct system.

(K) Oven - Most of the estate's bread was baked in this oven. The baker filled the large chamber with wood and charcoal, and then lit it. When only the hot coals remained, he raked the embers through the grating into the ash box below. Dough was then placed in the hot oven, and soon sent the delicious aroma of baking bread through the air.

(L) Detention Cell - A chain and pair of handcuffs were found fastened to a post in the left corner of this small chamber, making the room's use as a cell a good guess. The drawings of schooners and a street scene may well date to Danish times. Adjacent to the cell there was once a sick house with a cistern. At Annaberg only one or two overseers were responsible for controlling a large enslaved labor population. Tensions often ran high. Desertions were also common. Force was seen as the necessary deterrent; punishments such as detainment were dealt out liberally by the overseers. For more serious offenses, the local judge in Cruz Bay was empowered, and indeed mandated by law, to take harsher measures.

(M) Building Materials - Notice the rough fragments of volcanic rock used in the construction of this building. The rocks are set in a mortar consisting of sand, fresh water, molasses, and lime. Where arches and corners called for square or special shaped stones, both coral and bricks were used. Brain coral was very popular because it could be cut and shaped easily when it was first taken from the

HIKING TRAILS

sea and was still soft. Red and yellow bricks came from Europe as ballast on ships.

(N) Firing Tunnels - Here workers fed bagasse to the two furnace tunnels that heated the boiling bench above. At one time, a chimney was located at the center of the "firing trench." It provided the draft necessary to pull the fire into the tunnels and under the coppers above.

(O) Rum Still - Originally two 250-gallon stills stood at this location. A portion of fermented liquid, consisting of a mixture of molasses, water, and skimmings (from the top of boiling coppers), was taken from the butts and placed in the stills and boiled. The mixture turned to steam, which was then passed through cool water, which in turn condensed the steam into alcohol. It was important to keep the water in the cooling cistern cool or the steam could not be properly condensed. The water for the Annaberg cooling cistern was kept constantly cool thanks to the implementation of an aqueduct system that carried water to the cooling cistern by gravity from a water supply located on the hill above the factory. Raw rum ("kill-devil") was cured in barrels where it mellowed and was made ready for export. Approximately 30% of a sugar factory's profit was derived from rum production.

Typical 19-Century Rum Still, Artist Unknown, Courtesy NPS, PD

(P) Mule Pound - Mules were typically used for work, along with horses and donkeys, on sugar plantations. The park service has now allowed agricultural enthusiasts to use this area for growing local plants such as coconuts, bamboo, sugar cane, bananas, and papayas.

Annaberg Note: Some description related to the factory layout above (especially the relationship and function of F, G, H, I,) is credited to research conducted and generously shared by David W. Knight Sr. in his 2002 publication, *Understanding Annaberg: A Brief History of Estate Annaberg on St. John, U.S. Virgin Islands,* pp. 25-27. We are indebted to the author for his valuable historical account of this major cultural landmark on St. John as well as for information published by the NPS.

(10) Leinster Bay Trail (0.8 miles, 30 minutes)
Difficulty: Easy

Follows the old Danish Road eastward along the seashore from Annaberg to Waterlemon Bay. Connects with *#11 Johnny Horn Trail* at the east end of the shore, which in turn connects with *#12 Brown Bay Trail* 0.6 miles from Waterlemon Bay. The beach at the end of the Leinster Bay Trail is small but good for swimming. There is excellent snorkeling around Waterlemon Cay. (See *Beaches, #10 Leinster/Waterlemon Cay Beach, p. 166.*)

Land records dating back to the early eighteenth century show parcels being acquired here by French Huguenots. In the early years of colonization, Danes had trouble enticing their citizens to settle in these islands. To help populate their colonies, they adopted a policy of open colonization, which permitted French, Dutch, and English settlers to acquire land on the Danish possessions. Behind the beach, you'll find ruins of a former sugar works. In the mid-1800s, the land was owned by an Irishman, James Murphy. He acquired the property along with Annaberg and several other large land tracts in the area. Murphy was a wealthy merchant. At one point he had the largest sugar plantation on St. John. On the shore at Leinster Bay, Murphy constructed various support facilities, including a warehouse, carpentry and blacksmith shops, and a sugar factory to process cane. At the top of the hill above Leinster Bay, Murphy built a great house from which he took pleasure in surveying his vast holdings. The foundation and part of the main floor are still in place. The views from the great house are stunning.

(11) Johnny Horn Trail. (1.8 miles, 2 hours)
Difficulty: Strenuous

This trail can be accessed from three points—Leinster Bay *(#10 Leinster Bay Trail),* Coral Bay at Moravian Church (see note below) or Borck Bay, East End *(#12 Brown Bay Trail).*

Old Danish Lookout

If accessing from the Moravian Church in Coral Bay, you might want to park your vehicle near the church and continue the rest of the way up the hill on foot. The paved road quickly turns into a very steep dirt road, which is difficult to traverse without an off-road vehicle equipped with 4-wheel drive.

When accessing the Johnny Horn Trail from *#10 Leinster Bay Trail,* you'll first come to the ruins of an old Danish lookout, less than a 10-minute walk up the hill from the beach. The structure was originally built as a custom's house, but sentries also kept watch from here for runaways attempting to gain freedom by swimming to nearby Tortola, in the BVI. (Abolition came about in the British West Indies in 1833; on St. John not until 1848.)

A short distance above the lookout on Windy Hill you reach the remains of what's left of the James Murphy great house. His once grand domain was known for its extensive library and fine mahogany furnishings. The inscription on the wall dates the property at 1806. James Murphy died in 1810 and is buried in a nearby cemetery. At the beginning of the twentieth century the house was used as a guest house. At one point, it also served as a home for delinquent boys.

(12) Brown Bay Trail (1.6 miles, 2 hours)
Difficulty: Strenuous

The *#11 Johnny Horn Trail* connects with the Brown Bay Trail about 0.6 miles from Waterlemon Bay. At this juncture one can either exit the Johnny Horn Trail and follow the Brown Bay Trail to its entrance on Route 10 at Borck Creek, East End or continue southward and eventually reach Coral Bay at the Emmaus Moravian Church.

Taking the Borck Creek Access to the Brown Bay Trail–The Brown Bay Trail entrance at Borck Creek is reached by vehicle when traveling east from Coral Bay on Route 10. It begins up the dirt road just past the concrete bridge, which is about a mile from the Emmaus Moravian Church. There is usually room for parking at the beginning of the dirt road.

Walking a short distance up the dirt road you come to a metal gate leading to the Virgin Islands National Park firing range. The Brown Bay Trail begins at the start of the path to the right of the gate. A few yards from the gate, you come to the Hermitage ruins on the right-hand side of the path. The ruins include storage buildings and a cistern. Not much has been documented about the historical use of these buildings, however, they are obviously quite old and their proximity and potential access to the bay suggest the possibility of some form of commercial enterprise.

Continuing on, the trail then ascends through hot, dry scrub to a ridge overlooking Hurricane Hole to the south after which it descends the north side of the hill through much more pleasant dry forest vegetation. At the bottom of the main trail is a path leading to a small cemetery encircled by a metal fence. Note the touching tombstone inscription memorializing James Thomas Abbot Davis written by the bereaved mother of the twenty-year-old son who was buried here in 1860.

The beach at Brown Bay is a good spot to pause for a swim. There are sandbars that extend well out into the water, making it ideal for wading. Close to the beach there is a good deal of grassy vegetation. The seagrass bed provides a favored habitat for conch. The beach is often deserted. Enjoy good snorkeling on the right side.

At the western end of the Brown Bay Beach are early colonial ruins dating to the 1720s. Portions of this area played a key role as an initial staging point for rebels at the start of the 1733 rebellion. An 1804 probate inventory shows a large complex existing at this location and a dwelling house on the hillside. Other buildings included a boiling house, smoke house, distillery, and basement with built-in sugar kettles. There was also a horsemill, privy, and housing for enslaved laborers. With the exception of the beachfront factory ruins, easily found at the end of the beach, most of the other buildings lay buried beneath the bush and are difficult to reach.

South Shore

(13) Salt Pond Bay Trail (0.2 miles, 15 minutes)
Difficulty: Moderate
Trail begins at the parking area 3.9 miles south of Coral Bay. Hike the graded trail down to Salt Pond Bay Beach and picnic area through arid, cactus, scrub land.

(14) Drunk Bay Trail (0.3 miles, 20 minutes)
Difficulty: Easy
Walk to the southeast end of Salt Pond Bay Beach and turn east. The trail skirts the north side of a salt pond, which is good for viewing wading birds. Some residents harvest the accumulated salt during May and June. Note the windswept, stunted plant growth as you approach the rocky Drunk Bay shoreline.

(15) Ram Head Trail (1.0 miles, 1 hour)
Difficulty: Strenuous
Trail starts at the southeast end of Salt Pond Bay Beach. This rocky, exposed pathway leads to a blue cobble beach and then to switchbacks and finally up the hillside to its crest 200 feet above the Caribbean, where you will find magnificent windswept scenery. Maroons took refuge in this area during the Danish colonial era to live off the abundance of fish that could be caught near shore. Certain varieties of cactus supplied liquids and edible fruit.

(16) Tektite Trail (0.7 miles, 1 hour)
Difficulty: Strenuous

The name commemorates the scientific experiments conducted by aquanauts in 1969 on Great Lameshur Bay, which can be seen from various points along the trail. The trail starts 60 feet west of the top of the steep, concrete-paved hill. It overlooks the bay below and is marked by a sign. There is usually room to park on the flat, grassy area located a few feet below the trailhead entrance. The path takes you into the woods and along the west side of the peninsula running along the bay. At the start, it climbs steeply up to a ridge where it meets an old bulldozed road. It then follows the route along the ridge over three hills, with superb views of Ram Head and Lameshur Bay. Just after you pass the top of the third hill, a side trail on the left leads out to Cabritte Horn Point. (To facilitate locating the entrance to the side trail, you may find a makeshift stone marker signaling the trail junction). The Cabritte Trail Spur gets little maintenance, so the going could be rough.

   Moving on, the main trail continues down the hill where it terminates at a ledge with great views of the bay and Yawzi Point. There is no easy or safe way down from the ledge. Rather than attempt the climb, return to your starting point by retracing your steps and hiking back up the trail.

View from the Tektite Trail

(17) Yawzi Point Trail (0.3 miles, 20 minutes)
Difficulty: Easy

Located on the peninsula between Great Lameshur Bay and Little Lameshur Bay, this trail offers visitors a pleasant hike and nice scenery. The entrance to the trailhead is off a dirt road leading to the Virgin Islands Experimental Research Station (VIERS). It's marked by a pair of signs pointing left to both the Yawzi Point Trail and the VIERS waterfront facility. The Yawzi Point trailhead is a short drive down the dirt road and is marked by a sign on the right. It offers views of both Great Lameshur and Little Lameshur bays. Along the path you can find ruins of homes from the Danish colonial period. Here persons afflicted with yaws disease were once quarantined and required to live. Small rocky beaches can be accessed by side trails, which serve as good snorkel entry points.

(18) Bordeaux Mountain Trail
& (19) Bordeaux Peak Spur Trail (1.5 miles, 1 hour)
Difficulty: Strenuous

The Bordeaux Mountain Trail follows an old road and begins near the ranger residence about 1,000 feet up the steep hill at the west end of Little Lameshur Bay Road. The trail climbs 1,100 feet to Bordeaux Mountain Road. Centerline Road is 1.7 miles to the northwest of this junction. A short distance northwest of the junction is the short Bordeaux Peak Spur Trail on the left that takes you a few feet higher to the very top of the mountain. There are no views, just the satisfaction of knowing that you have hiked to elevation 1,200 feet and have probably reached the highest point on the island.

(20) Lameshur Bay Trail (1.5 miles, 1.25 hours)
Difficulty: Moderate

Trail connects Lameshur Bay with Reef Bay Trail. Open dry-forest hiking. A short distance from the trail entrance is a path leading to the hillside overlooking Europa Bay. A little further on, a second spur leads 0.3 miles to a salt pond trail and the coral rubble beach at Europa Bay.

STJ ON FOOT AND BY CAR

L'Esperance Ruins

Centerline

(21) L'Esperance Trail (2.6 miles, 2.5 hours to Reef Bay) Difficulty: Strenuous Begins at the Centerline Road trail marker, located just past Estate Catherineberg. It ultimately descends to Reef Bay Trail following the old Sieben Road, a major thoroughfare in Danish colonial times. There is a connection off the Reef Bay Trail that allows hikers to walk all the way to Lameshur Bay. (See *Reef Bay Trail map, p. 146.*) The L'Esperance portion of the trail takes you to the L'Esperance ruins followed by the Sieben-Mollendahl ruins, where you'll find St. John's only baobab, or "spirit" tree.

Immediately to the left of the main entrance to the L'Esperance Trail there's an observation platform which, if open, offers nice views of the valley below.

The distance to the L'Esperance ruins is less than 0.3 miles from the start of the trail. L'Esperance was formed in 1736 with the merger of two properties having original land grants dating 1720 and 1721. L'Esperance and the early plantations of Sieben and Mollendahl were landlocked, making it costly for the owners of these two plantations to reach the sea for shipping, which ultimately became a contributing factor to the abandonment of sugar cultivation at this location.

The entrance to L'Esperance is marked by a bridge spanning the gut with a path leading up to the plantation buildings. Behind the buildings are graves, one marking the resting place of Henrick Tunis, 1733–1756, and the other of Louise Sommer, deceased 1861.

Estate Sieben ruins are approximately 0.7 miles beyond L'Esperance. They are reached via a couple of spur paths leading off to the west on the right side of the main trail. The spur paths are not well maintained and are often difficult to find. Keep a sharp eye out, and look for home-made stone markers, often placed on the ground by fellow hikers to signal entrances to the paths. The first path leads directly into the Sieben ruins and the baobab tree. The second is a bit more circuitous.

In time the Sieben plantation was merged with the adjacent Mollendahl Plantation and became Sieben-Mollendahl. Earlier, Mollendahl had itself been enlarged by its merger with two other plantations. By 1793 Sieben-Mollendahl as well as L'Esperance and parts of Reef Bay were under a single

Baobab "Spirit Tree" at Sieben

ownership. The original Sieben plantation buildings were largely destroyed by a hurricane in the late 1830s. When rebuilt, many sections of original structures of the sugar works were assimilated into living quarters and other adaptive reuses.

A few yards south of the ruins stands a massive baobab tree.

This baobab or "spirit tree" is thought to be the only one in existence on St. John.

The African baobab *(Adansonia digitata)* is the most widespread tree species of its genus. Some speculate that the St. John tree may have been secretly carried to the island as a young plant (or fertilized seed) by an enslaved African. The long-lived baobabs are commonly found on the hot, arid savannas of Africa. Their highly unusual bottle-shaped base can store huge amounts of water. Their life span is the subject of some debate. Radiocarbon dating suggest the oldest living baobab may have been 1,275 years old. However, there's speculation by some that these trees can live for more than 3,000 years. The baobab typically bears very large, white flowers with many stamens. They usually open in the late afternoon and stay open for just 24 hours. At first blooming, they have a sweet scent, which quickly becomes stinky as they turn brown and fall from the tree. The opening at the base of many baobab trees is often so large that the tree is sometimes used for personal shelter as well as for commercial purposes. In South Africa there is reportedly a bar located inside a baobab's trunk.

The leaves, fruit, and bark of the tree have for centuries been used in Africa as a food source and a natural remedy for the treatment of a variety of ailments. Today, the pulp of the fruit is being ground into a powder and widely marketed as an abundant source of vitamin C, calcium, iron, potassium, and magnesium.

Many believe the baobab has supernatural powers and is thought to be a haven for spirits. In Africa it was often used as a gathering place for important tribal meetings. The tree is associated with many superstitions and legends. Along the Zambezi, tribes pass down popular stories of a time when the baobabs became too upright and proud, so the gods became angry and uprooted the trees, and then threw them back in the ground upside down. In the Kafue National Park, there is a baobab known as "Kondanamwali," which translates to "tree that eats maidens." Legend has it that the tree fell in love with four beautiful maidens. When they reached puberty, the maidens made the tree jealous by finding husbands. One night during a thunderstorm the tree cunningly opened and lured the maidens inside, offering shelter. Once inside, they re-

HIKING TRAILS 145

mained forever trapped. Apparently, the captive maidens can still be heard crying on stormy nights. Once thought to be a myth, some doctors and scientists are now affirming that consumption of the baobab's leaves, fruit, or bark will enhance fertility in women.

Some aspects of the baobabs reproductive cycle are not yet fully understood. The existence of isolated trees like this baobab may be due to self-incompatibility or an inability to reproduce without a partnering tree.

Returning to the main pathway, you may elect either to continue your walk downward through the forested woodlands of Mollendahl to Reef Bay and eventually proceed on to Lameshur Bay, or you can reverse course at this point, and head back up the trail to Centerline Road.

(22) Reef Bay Trail, (2.2 miles, 2.0 hours) NPS, Self-Guided Trail Difficulty: Strenuous

A trip to St. John seems somehow incomplete without an invigorating hike down the Reef Bay Trail. The trail descends 937 feet through moist and dry forests, traversing four sugar estates (Old Works, Hope, Jossie Gut, and Par Force) before arriving at the ruins of the Reef Bay sugar works near the

Reef Bay Trailhead

beach at Genti Bay. Reef Bay was the last operating sugar mill on St. John. It was converted to steam power in 1855. Much of the sugar-processing machinery is still intact.

A highlight of the hike is a visit to St. John's famous petroglyphs, or rock carvings, at a freshwater pool hidden deep in the forest. Most of the carved images are thought to be the handiwork of Taino/Arawak Indians, who lived here until around 1500 A.D. However, some speculate that a few of the drawings may have been done by runaways in hiding during the Revolt of 1733.

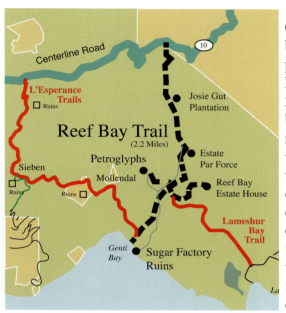

The hike from Centerline Road to the beach at Reef Bay is pleasant. All downhill! It takes about 2 hours to reach the beach. Park service markers along the way identify many of the exotic plants and other points of interest. The markers are capitalized and shown in bold typeface in this text for ease of reader identification. (See our *Checklist of Trees, Plants, and Cacti, pp. 197-217,* for plants not identified by markers along the trail.)

To avoid the strenuous walk back up, you can take the hike under the supervision of a park ranger and have the option of returning by boat to Cruz Bay. Check with the park service at the visitor center in Cruz Bay for reservations. Bring water and wear comfortable walking shoes, not sandals. The beach at Genti Bay is excellent for swimming and a picnic lunch.

Getting Started

Descending the trail, you'll become immediately aware of the dense vegetation growing along the path. This part of the trail can get very damp and is dominated by larger trees—kapoks, mangoes, locusts, turpentines, and tamarinds. There are over 1,000 varieties of flora on St. John. Some flora is indigenous, but many plants came from other lands, carried here on ocean currents, others blown here by the wind, and still others carried as unofficial passengers on merchant ships or by enslaved people transported from Africa.

Plants supplied food for animals and people. Some were used as building materials and many were fashioned into household implements. Fishermen used plants to craft fish traps and nets, while some plants were used in local industries like basketmaking.

A few yards from the start of the trail you'll come to an informational plaque describing **ANTHURIUMS**. Anthuriums are perennials that grow on the ground or up in trees. Local varieties found in abundance along the trail are *Anthurium acaule* (scrub brush) and *Anthurium cordatum* (heart leaf). Both are foliage species and are not of the flowering group of anthuriums. Scrub brush has long green leaves with seasonal red fruit. Dead leaves form a lacy skeleton, which was once used locally to scrub pots and pans. Heart-leaf anthurium produces beautiful foliage that sometimes is home for nests of Jack Spaniards (wasps with very painful bites!) and tree snails. The pistil of this plant is a long, rough, green whip.

Walking a few minutes further on, you reach a marker describing **BAY RUM TREES**. This tree with its oil-laden, dark-green leaves was once of economic importance to St. John. From the leaves, bay oil was extracted to make bay rum cologne. This was done from the 1890s until the 1940s. The bay rum tree is an evergreen and is sometimes called "wild cinnamon." They still flourish on Bordeaux Mountain and behind Cinnamon Bay.

Termite Nest

A short distance ahead is a **DRAINAGE GUTTER**. Despite the passage of time, running water, and the pounding of feet, hooves, and wheels, roads like this one have lasted due to good drainage design and respect for the contours of this steep island. This road gutter carried water across the road and not down it. In some places, paving with flat, volcanic rock was used to support heavy carts laden with hogsheads of sugar.

Next comes a **WEST INDIAN LOCUST**. The West Indian locust produces shiny, brown, thick-walled pods, 2-5 inches long. The pods contain a sweet, tan, mealy powder, which tastes good, but smells bad. Giant locusts on the Reef Bay Trail produce thousands of these free candy bars each year.

Along the trail you'll likely see many woodland creatures, including lizards, hermit crabs, spiders, and of course, the ubiquitous wild donkey. Bats, mongooses, and many other critters live here as well.

The huge, ball-like houses seen dangling from tree trunks are built by termites. Termites do not kill living trees, even though they often use them to support their homes. These blind insects access wood on the ground and elsewhere by traveling through tunnels and following one another's scent.

Kapok Tree

After descending some steep stone steps, you'll come to a **KAPOK OR SILK COTTON TREE**. Notice how broken or cut-off limb stubs have healed over—a good protection against infection and decay. Planters and enslaved persons slept on mattresses stuffed with fluffy, silk-cotton fiber from the seed pods. Centuries ago, Taino/Arawak and Carib families migrated through the islands in huge dugout *ceibas* (or boats) made of the balsa-like wood. The buttressed root system may be another adaptation to help provide moisture and support for mature trees.

On St. John many plants were used in folk or bush medicines to treat a variety of ailments. For example, aloe vera, commonly found along the Reef Bay Trail, was used in the treatment of colds, asthma, ulcers, burns, and insect bites. The leaf of the plant can also be split in two, and the jelly extracted and applied to the face to remove wrinkles. Congo root was used for stomach aches. Hog plums were frequently chewed as a way of clearing the throat of mucus. Ginger Thomas was used for a variety of maladies, including headaches, colds, fever, diabetes, and jaundice. Wild maran was used as a remedy for headaches, the noni plant as a painkiller, and turpentine for a sore back. Soursop leaves were often boiled, and the liquid served as a sedative. Soursop tea is today thought by many to act as a cancer cure and preventative. (Photos of these medicinal plants can be found in our *Checklist of Trees, Plants, and Cacti,* pp. 197-217.)

Walking on a few minutes further, you come to a **GENIP TREE**. A native of South America, this evergreen produces a tartly sweet fruit enjoyed by Virgin Islanders. The bark is smooth with a mottled, gray-green appearance formed by lichen. The leaves have a winged-leaf stem. Green fruit matures from June to September and has an edible pulp and seed. Genips ("keneps") blossom in late spring with star bursts of tiny, white, vanilla-scented flowers.

A 10-minute walk further, the path starts to descend downward towards Jossie Gut, eventually crossing over and passing the ruins of old plantation buildings on the right. Structures visible in the area include a horsemill and sugar factory where coppers (boiling kettles) were once located. Take a moment to read the **JOSSIE GUT SUGAR ESTATE** marker describing building materials that were employed to build these sturdy, colonial structures. A good lesson in learning how to make do with what's at hand.

A short distance ahead, you will find a marker identifying a **LIME TREE**. This thorny tree is a native of southern Asia. Lime trees were cultivated here for export years ago. They grow wild in Reef Bay, and the fruit normally matures during the "winter" months. Limes have many uses. Sailors prevented scurvy by adding limes to their diet. You can brew a bush tea by using three leaves each of lime and black wattle plus one bay leaf and a little sugar. Lime juice is also good for dissolving sea urchin spines or healing sandfly bites.

The trail continues, eventually crossing back over the gut, and then brings you to a **MANGO TREE** marker. This large tree is over 100 years old. The mango was introduced here in the eighteenth century from Asia. It's an evergreen that produces a yellow green, sweet-tasting, pear-shaped fruit in the late spring. The mango is first peeled and then eaten raw or stewed and made into a preserve.

About 0.25 miles further on you arrive at the remains of what was once part of the **PAR FORCE VILLAGE**. Par Force is a colonial plantation that was in existence as early as 1780. One of the estate's first recorded owners was Anthony Zytzema. Following his death, the property changed hands several times until it was finally purchased around 1830 by John Vetters, a man of substantial wealth. Vetters also acquired Reef Bay Estate, which was then a small tract of land skirting the beach. The two estates, Par Force and Reef Bay, were merged into a much larger Reef Bay Estate. Vetters had a new sugar factory constructed on the beach to replace operations at the Old Par Force factory.

In 1855 the plantation was sold to O.J. Bergeest and Company. It was during Bergeest's ownership that steam power was installed at the Reef Bay factory. William Marsh acquired the property in 1864 and profitably ran the plantation for the next fifty years, despite increasing labor costs and declining interest in West Indian cane. Marsh died in 1909, and two of his four daughters managed to keep producing sugar until 1916 when the sugar mill was finally forced to shut down. Despite the end of sugar-cane cultivation, workers continued to raise cattle and cultivate crops here until the 1940s when the land was abandoned.

Leaving the village, the trail then crisscrosses the gut a couple of more times before arriving at a junction with another path leading off to the right towards the petroglyphs, St. John's renowned rock carvings, only 0.3 miles away.

Petroglyphs

Most of these carvings are now believed to be the work of Taino/Arawak people. Some of the carvings are located above a reflection pool of water and were thought to be symbols for "water." A new petroglyph was found in 2011 when it was noticed that an old park photograph showed there was a petroglyph unaccounted for. The newest found symbol is thought to be thousands of years old, dating back to pre-Columbian times. The petroglyph site was listed on the National Register of Historic Places on July 7, 1982. The 60-foot waterfall, which is not stream fed and only flows during rainy season, is thought to have once been a sacred meet-

Molly Stevens, Courtesy Wikimedia under creative commons license,
https://commons.wikimedia.org/wiki/File:Petroglyphsstjohnusvi.jpg

ing place where religious rites were practiced, possibly by Taino/Arawaks. Fresh-water crayfish and algae can sometimes be seen in the pool at the foot of the waterfall.

Once back on the main trail, you cross the gut and come to a sign indicating directions to Europa Point Trail and Lameshur Bay. This is also the way to the Reef Bay Estate House. The path to the estate house is sometimes overgrown and difficult to follow, but if you are dressed properly and have the extra energy, you should be able to find your way safely up the steep hillside to the well-preserved ruins of this former residence.

To reach the estate house, start out by following the trail toward Lameshur Bay *(#20 Lameshur Bay Trail)*. The path quickly divides, about 0.3 miles from its starting point. Continue to the left. A little further ahead, there is a second split in the trail. Stay to the right, heading up the hill, and you eventually reach the estate house.

Reef Bay Estate House

The Reef Bay (or "Par Force") Estate House was built in 1832 and renovated in 1844. In 1994 the park service began restoring the house, but work was never completed. Like most great houses, the Reef Bay Estate House was built on a hilltop to take advantage of cool ocean breezes. The house is a significant architectural landmark. Author Paul Brooks shares a lyrical (if not somewhat eerie) impression upon his arrival at the great house, ca. 1970:

After a long descension on a perfectly constructed and still sound road, and a twenty-minute steep climb up the valley wall, we emerged into an overgrown clearing from the midst of which rose a graceful, almost elegant building....

Only the Estate House itself was still standing, but one could reconstruct the outbuildings from the patterns of the walls: servants' quarters, stables, kitchen, the last with a huge bake oven, door intact, ready for baking. To reconstruct the way of life that went on in the main house was more difficult, though the empty shell was full of murmurs.... twin flights of graceful curved steps mounting to the columned portico, stuccoed brick walls of a pinkish white, screened balconies. One corner of the house was hidden in a mass of color where flowering vines from the garden had run rampant, and out of the roof grew a fair-sized tree. The front door swung open, banging in the breeze.... A lizard welcomed us in. The cool green walls stopped short of the ceiling like a crypt, smelling of dust and damp stone. It was utterly silent except for a weird clicking sound, which I later learned was made by a gecko lizard. Broken shutters, empty rum bottles, and other rubbish lay about from the last high tide this family was to know. But what intrigued me was the coffin in the corner. No simple pine box, but the classic hexagonal pattern with sloping cover, obviously a fine piece of cabinet work, and judging from its size, designed for a woman. When I opened the lid, I found a purple lining, the rich tone undimmed by contact with light and air. - **(Courtesy Paul Brooks, appeared as article entitled "Beachcombing in the Virgin Islands," by Paul Brooks. Copyright 1960** *Harper's Magazine.* **All Rights reserved. Reproduced from the December 1960 issue by special permission.)**

William Marsh operated the sugar factory and lived in the house with his family until his death in 1909. The main building is usual-

Jack Boucher, Courtesy Wikimedia and Library of Congress, PD, https://www.loc.gov/resource/hhh. vi0011.photos/?sp=2

ly boarded up to prevent vandalism, but visitors may freely wander about the grounds. At the rear of the building are the ruins of the stable and outhouse. The structure to the right of the gate is a cookhouse.

In 1855 the house is believed to have been the residence of

the fifty-six-year-old widower, Stapleton Smith, and members of his family. Elizabeth, age nineteen, was a Moravian servant in the household of Smith. She and Henry Knevels, twenty-five years of age, a member of a prominent Dutch Reformed family, were lovers during Henry's five years as overseer at Par Force. After leaving Par Force and taking a position as overseer at the Caneel Bay Plantation, Elizabeth attempted to join Henry, but Smith twice denied her a pass to leave, despite a law allowing servants to annually make the election to switch employers. The couple made a heart-rendering appeal to the local judge who upheld Smith's denial, demonstrating the lingering frustrations and disappointments experienced by freed captives in the years immediately following Emancipation. As a result of conflicting regulations, it appears Smith also had the right to withhold the passport of an employee, which the judge seemed to agree trumped the law allowing servants the right to annually make the election to leave an employer. Census records suggest the two lovers were never officially united.

Mlogic, Courtesy Wikimedia under GNU free documentation and creative commons licenses, https://es.wikipedia.org/wiki/Archivo:Sansevieria_trifasciata_flower.jpg

Leaving the estate house, find your way back down the path to the main trail, and resume your hike toward the Reef Bay factory on the beach, 0.8 miles away.

Valley Floor

The path from here to the beach is flat. The environment on the valley floor is considerably drier than along upper portions of the trail. Early residents planted several varieties of citrus trees along the path. You can still spot lime trees close to the edge of the trail. A short distance ahead you come to a NPS marker for **WILD PINEAPPLE**. The plant was used as barrier hedges and living pasture fences. Despite its thick, thorny leaves, the plant yields a tasty fruit rich in Vitamin C.

The next marker identifies **SANSEVIERIA**. *Sansevieria* is a genus of about 70 species of flowering plants native to Africa, Madagascar, and southern Asia. Common names include mother-in-law's tongue, devil's tongue, bow string hemp, snake plant, and snake tongue. The flowers of the species are usually greenish-white, also rose, lilac-red, or brownish, produced on a simple or branched raceme. The fruit is a red or orange berry. In nature, they are pollinated by moths, but both flowering and fruiting are erratic, and few seeds are produced. This decorative plant is popular in the United States and Europe.

Note the marshy area on the left side of the trail. The numerous holes in the ground are made by land crabs, once highly sought by locals for food. After being trapped, the crabs were placed in a pen and fed a cleansing diet of cornmeal and coconut to ensure all impurities were removed before cooking them for dinner. Due to their dwindling numbers, catching land crabs is now prohibited.

Just before reaching the Reef Bay ruins, you'll pass the connecting L'Esperance Trail. (See *Hiking Trails, #21 L'Esperance Trail, p. 142.*)

Factory Building Looking Across Original Horsemill

Reef Bay Sugar Mill

Here the sugar industry died twice. The empty rooms and stone corrals contain overlapping ruins from two different eras. The Reef Bay mill was built around 1830. Originally, enslaved laborers brought bundles of cane to the horsemill, where they were crushed by animal-powered rollers to release the cane juice for processing. In 1861, after Denmark had abolished the practice of enslaved labor and St. John's other mills began to collapse, Reef Bay's new owners attempted to revive the dying industry by installing steam power to crush the cane. The old mill was enlarged and modernized. In 1863 the property was acquired by William Marsh, who managed to run the mill profitably for many years. However, exhausted soil and mainland sugar beets eventually helped halt St. John sugar production. Reef Bay was the last operating sugar mill on the island.

Reef Bay is one of the best examples of a sugar factory still standing on St. John. Visible for viewing and graphically identified on the pictured plaque in front of the main building (and named here in bold type) are the following components: **Steam-Power Equipment** installed in 1861 and located in the **Steam House** ("engine room") on the southwest side of the factory next to the grinding platform; steam-powered **Shaft and Gears** on the exterior side of the engine room wall, which turned the **Crushing Rollers** mounted on the grinding platform on the south side of the factory building where raw cane stalks were fed through the steam-powered rollers to release the cane juice; an **Animal-Powered Horsemill** from colonial plantation times prior to steam (positioned at the center of the grinding platform); a plantation-era **Gutter** that ran along the top of the grinding platform and channeled cane juice into the **Boiling House** where the cane juice was ladled from one of five boiling coppers to the next to release moisture (coppers were heated by spent, dried cane stalks—nothing was wasted); a **Curing House** on the northwest side of the factory building where hogsheads of crystallized brown sugar (muscovado) were stored to cure and drain off any remaining moisture; and a **Rum Still** on the north side of the building where all the drippings from the sugar production process were boiled and distilled

Steam House Equipment

Boiling Bench

Steam-Powered Gears, Shaft, and Rollers

Coppers

into rum.

After cane was cut and processed in the factory, it was shipped to Europe on sailing vessels. Dories were used to transport the sugar from the shore to waiting vessels. The dories were tipped on their sides to permit the heavy hogsheads (each one weighing about 1,600 pounds) to be rolled inside. When the dories reached the ships, the hogsheads had to be lifted aboard and then stored.

Take time to explore the beach and enjoy a swim. If you are making the hike back up the trail to Centerline, it's best to leave yourself two or three daylight hours to reach the top.

(23) Great Sieben Trail (0.5 miles, 25 minutes)
Difficulty: Moderate

This follows the remnants of an old colonial road from Fish Bay up to the L'Esperance Trail, passing through the Sieben ruins and past an ancient baobab tree along the way. From the Fish Bay area, the entrance to the trail is located by driving up Cocolobo Trail off Marina Drive. At the "T" turn right and go up the hill a short distance to a point near the top of the hill where another road comes down to meet it. Take a left onto this road and follow up to the first sharp turn. The trail starts next to the power pole at the turn.

Beaches

St. John's shoreline offers visitors a rich and bountiful array of dazzling beaches with fringing reefs and seagrass beds for swimming and snorkeling. However, defining the "best" is highly subjective, based on factors such as individual snorkeling/swimming abilities, water and wind conditions, and the marine life particular to a given site. Below is a list of some of the most popular and accessible beaches and snorkeling spots. Park rangers at the visitor center can also advise as to which beaches and snorkeling spots might best meet your interest and level of expertise. All beaches in the Virgin Islands are open to the public provided they are reached using public roads or trails or you arrive by water, and do not cross private property. (*Our list numbers each beach, and its corresponding location can be found numbered in yellow on our centerfold map.*)

North Shore

(1) Honeymoon Beach
Accessed at three points: the Lind Point Trail from behind the park service visitor center; upper Lind Point Trail entrance located on North Shore Road just outside Cruz Bay; and Caneel Bay Resort.

Honeymoon Beach

(See *Hiking Trails, #1 Lind Point Trail, p. 116.*) Lovely sandy beach ideal for swimming and snorkeling. In the clear waters off the point on the west side of the beach, you'll find brain corals, lettuce leaf, elkhorn, and even some pillar corals. A narrow but diverse reef grips the shoreline from the end of Honeymoon eastward to Caneel Bay. Abundant finger corals are present. Plentiful fish. Popular destination for charter boats. Watersports equipment and beach chairs available for rent. You can also purchase sandwiches, ice cream, beer, wine, and rum drinks at the beach bar next to the water. Public restrooms are available.

(2) Caneel Bay Resort Beach

Classic white-sand beach located in front of the main reception area of the resort. Water is generally calm and easy for wading or swimming. Starting about 100 feet out and hugging the

Fred Hsu, Courtesy Wikimedia under GNU free documentation and creative commons licenses, https://commons.wikimedia.org/wiki/File:Caneel_Bay_Boat_Mary_II_at_Caneel_Beach.jpg

shore in 10 feet or less depth, are diminutive hard corals as well as gorgonians that shelter diverse fish populations—largely juveniles. (See *North Shore Motor Tour, Caneel Bay Plantation, pp. 63-64.*)

(3) Hawksnest Beach

Favorite swimming beach. Attracts locals and visitors alike. Beautiful white-sandy expanse. There are long fingers of a reef that extend perpendicularly from the sandy beach. Much of this area is too shallow to safely snorkel above the reef and must be viewed from the sides. Water can get rough during winter months. Stingrays and turtles are frequently seen. There are restrooms, changing rooms, pavilions, charcoal grills, and picnic areas. Plenty of parking.

Hawksnest Beach

(4) Gibney-Oppenheimer Beach

Pretty little beach. Famous scientist and "father of the atomic bomb," Robert Oppenheimer, once lived for brief periods of time on a portion of this beach with his wife and daughter. Oppenheimer appreciated the secluded refuge afforded by the island and the beach. His house was left to the people of the Virgin Islands by his daughter, Toni. Today the beach is maintained by the Virgin Islands government and is open to the public. For snorkelers, a few interesting clumps of reef follow the shoreline. (See *North Shore Tour, Gibney-Oppenheimer Beach, pp. 65-67.*)

(5) Jumbie Beach

Crescent-shaped beach accessed from North Shore Road. From the right side of the beach (if facing the water) a shallow reef extends, maze-like at first, all the way along the cliffs to Trunk Bay. The sandy bottom is eventually about 10 feet beneath you as you follow the reef. Other than a few elkhorn corals here and there, there's not much to see on the left side until you reach the point. Here various corals and other marine life extend down the underwater slope to about 20 feet.

Jumbie Beach

(6) Trunk Bay Beach

Stunning St. John beach. Most visited beach and one of the most beautiful on the island. In 1959, the park service purchased Trunk Bay from the Boulon family, who for many years ran their legendary guest house at this location. (See *North Shore Motor Tour, Trunk Bay Beach, pp. 68-71.*) Trunk Bay takes its name from the trunk turtle that once nested here. The park service maintains a

Trunk Bay Beach

snorkel trail (200 yards, 30 minutes) just a few yards offshore, which offers visitors a chance to explore the coral reef and identify various forms of reef life with the aid of underwater signage. The trail begins near the lifeguard station and follows the west side of Trunk Bay Cay for about 300 feet before making a U-turn back to the beach. Along the west side of the cay there are various sea fans, whips, and plumes, along with brain corals. There is an admission charge to access the beach. Lifeguard on duty. Snack bar, retail shop, picnic area, restrooms, and shower facilities. Snorkel gear is available for a small rental fee. Plenty of parking. Handicapped access.

(7) Cinnamon Bay Beach

Long white-sandy beach with plenty of shaded areas. Cinnamon Bay tends to be one of the windiest locations on the north shore, which can make for slow-going when snorkeling and getting into the water. Approaching the eastern side of Cinnamon Bay Cay, the undersides of a small low ridge, shelter fish, crabs, and other invertebrates; perhaps a lobster or two. Snappers and other reef fish inhabit the nooks and crannies of the cay's steep slopes and deeper waters on the east, north, and west sides. Here also are scattered large coral heads and sea fans. A few small pillar-coral formations adorn the northwest corner. Shallow sandy areas on the south side of the cay provide safe resting spots before returning to the beach. In the canyons of the mostly dead reef at the opposite (east) end of the beach are often plenty of fish. (For more information on Cinnamon Bay

Cinnamon Beach

see *North Shore Motor Tour, Cinnamon Bay, pp. 71-72,* and *Hiking Trails, #5 Cinnamon Bay Loop Trail, pp. 118-126.*)

(8) Maho Bay Beach

Crystal-clear, calm water, easy for snorkeling and swimming. Starfish and other marine life populate the bay. Pelicans dive for fish along the beach. There are seagrass beds in the middle stretches of the bay that provide a habitat for green turtles, typically seen more frequently in the early morning or late afternoon. There's limited coral and fish in the south-side waters (left side, if facing the water) of the beach. To the north, the reef is not especially thick or diverse, but supports abundant fish populations, including plenty of angel fish. Maho and adjacent Francis Bay are usually less affected by winter swells than elsewhere on the north shore, so the waters here are usually quite calm. Water sport amenities as well as food and drinks are available. Plenty of parking along the beach and in the lot at far north end of the beach. Popular anchorage for yachts. A perfect beach for families and children. While the beach itself is quite narrow, the white sand extends well out into the water and remains shallow. The shallowness often invites schools of small fry fish to congregate near shore. This tends to attract pelicans and brown boobies.

Maho Beach

(9) Francis Bay Beach

Sandy beach. A favorite for snorkeling where you can see eels, turtles, and other marine life. The calm waters contain schools of juvenile fish and small coral heads. For endurance swimmers, the first 0.33 miles of Mary Point peninsula's shoreline from the north end of the beach yields mostly gorgonians, tube sponges, and

Francis Bay Beach

patches of colonial anemones in about 10 feet of water. Beyond the point, scattered hard coral appear in deeper water. Use of a boat or kayak for longer distances is a good idea. Francis Bay is usually a good place to view sea turtles, pelicans, and large predator fish chasing schools of small "fry." The beach is reached either via the Francis Bay Trail, which begins to the right of the warehouse ruins next to the parking area at the western end of Mary Creek or by continuing to follow the road directly down to the beach, where it terminates. If you take this route, and it's a busy day, you may have to pull off and park well ahead of reaching the beach and go the remaining distance on foot. Just a few steps before reaching the beach, you'll spot a wooden path on the right leading off into the mangroves. Rather than accessing the beach at road's end, if you follow the path through the woodlands, you emerge at a less crowded area of the beach. The walkway also takes you past an observation platform at the edge of the salt pond where you can pause to view various water birds. (For more information see *Francis Bay Ruins, North Shore Tour, p. 126,* and *Hiking Trails, #7 Francis Bay Trail, pp. 79-82*.)

(10) Leinster/Waterlemon Cay Beach

A 10-minute walk from the parking lot at Annaberg brings you to a narrow stretch of sand where entry is gained to a shallow reef of coral heads sitting on a sandy bottom that is habitat for parrot fish, tangs, and grunts. Not far to seaward, is a steep drop off, where blue chromis, an occasional sea turtle, and gorgonians are seen. Ten minutes further down the trail (by the narrow hard-packed sand beach) a seagrass bed is close to the shore. Swimming over this or hugging the eastern shore and entering deeper water by climbing down rocks (not so easy), Waterlemon Cay is eventually reached. The cay is ringed with a comprehensive variety of fish, corals, and gorgonians. Seabirds are often perched on its shore. Although there's a strong current that runs on the Tortola side of the cay, you should be okay if you go with it and not against it, but only do so if you are confident about your swimming ability. A soft sandy spit of beach on the cay's southern tip offers a place to rest or warm up. Waterlemon is one of the few places on St. John that is home to orange cushion sea stars. It's also a good place to see sea turtles. At the end of the Leinster Bay Trail you'll find ruins in the bush behind the beach. (See *Hiking Trails, #10 Leinster Bay Trail, p. 136.*)

East End

(11) Brown Bay Beach

Accessible only by boat or trail from Waterlemon Bay or East End. (See *Hiking Trails, #10 Leinster Bay Trail, #11 Johnny Horn Trail, and #12 Brown Bay Trail, pp. 136-139.*) Remote Brown Bay has a sandy though narrow and often seaweed-strewn beach. Reasonable swimming, but not ideal. There's an extensive shallow seagrass bed, home to conch and other invertebrates. To the east are mostly gorgonians. To the west, towards Leinster Bay, the fringing reef is thick with seemingly every conceivable kind of flexible-skeleton gorgonian along with some hard corals, including staghorns and plenty of fish mixed in. There are also historic ruins in the bush at the far western end of the beach.

(12) Haulover Beach

Haulover Beach is on the south side of Haulover Bay, which is reached by a drive through the roller-coaster hills of East End. The waters are calm beyond the narrow sand and rubble beach. Snorkeling is relatively good at each end of the beach. Getting into the water can be difficult. It is rocky and those rocks are studded with painful sea urchins. Be careful! The beach is so named because at this location early residents pulled small vessels back and forth over this flat and narrow piece of land, which separates the Caribbean on one side from Drake's Passage on the other. It's a good beach for checking out a variety of shells. Watch for crabs darting in and out of their holes. The beach was featured in the 1988 movie, *"The Big Blue."* There's an informal path on the opposite (north) side of the road that leads to the rocky shore facing Tortola. Many of the star-coral boulders here have partially or fully died, but to the north and beyond the reef remains one of the densest live coral reefs around St. John. Often windy/choppy. Difficult to access water without proper footwear.

(13) Hansen Bay Beach and
(14) Saltwell Bottom Beach

Two popular, privately owned sandy beaches located on either side of the former schoolhouse overlooking White Bay. Snorkeling is good at both locations. Both beaches offer beach chairs and there are paddle boards and kayaks for rent. Parking is free, but a voluntary donation for the right to cross the property to access these beaches is always welcome.

South Shore

(15) Salt Pond Bay Beach

One of the nicest beaches on the south side of the island. Clear water with excellent snorkeling and swimming. Most snorkelers enjoy the west side of the beach. It's almost a quarter-mile swim to two sets of rocks breaking the water in the middle of the bay, but worth it for the health, diversity, and plenitude of hard corals, gorgonians, and fish there. Two popular walking trails start at the far end of the beach. The first skirts a salt pond and leads out to Drunk Bay;

Salt Pond Beach

the second involves a hardy hike out to Ram Head Point. The rock and shell art that spontaneously appears at the edge of the water at Drunk Bay is magical. Hikers will find the dramatic vistas from the top of Ram Head well worth the hike. (See *Hiking Trails, #13 Salt Pond Trail, #14 Drunk Bay Trail* and *#15 Ram Head Trail, p. 139.*) Picnic tables and restrooms are on the beach.

(16) Little Lameshur Beach
At the end of the south shore road from Coral Bay is a sheltered sand beach separated from a larger rocky beach (great Lameshur Bay) by the Yawzi Point peninsula. Nice beach for swimming and snorkeling. A small cluster of rocks protruding from the shallow water just off the beach to the west is dense with snappers, grunts,

and other fish—good beginner's spot. Otherwise, on rare calm days, the western shoreline all the way to Europa Bay is a visual delight of deep clefts and canyons with schools of fish in the water beneath you. Good opportunity to wander through the ruins of an old bay rum factory or take a short hike up the hill to the former residence of a young Danish Countess, who lived on St. John for a brief time. Ample parking next to the bay still ruins. However, only authorized vehicles permitted to use the steep road going up the hillside to the former residence of the countess. Best on foot.
(See *South Shore Motor Tour, Little Lameshur Bay, pp. 106-112*.)

(17) Genti Beach

Great spot for a refreshing dip following a hike down the Reef Bay Trail. Sandy beach with a few good areas for swimming. Ideal place for a picnic. Snorkeling is good along the shallow, grassy reef spanning the western shoreline of the bay. Small sharks and other predator fish are frequently spotted feeding along the reef, which also serves as a habitat for conch. Area attractions include the ruins of the Reef Bay sugar mill and estate house as well as Taino/Arawak rock carvings. (See *Hiking Trails, #22 Reef Bay Trail, pp. 145-157*.)

(18) Westin Resort Beach

About 2 miles south of Cruz Bay on Route 104 is the Westin Resort. The resort features a quarter-mile of white-sand beach. The

Westin Resort Beach

water is usually calm. There is a seagrass bed just offshore, which offers an opportunity to see small fish, occasional rays, and other marine life.

Checklist of Mammals, Reptiles, Amphibians, and Arthropods

Most of St. John's animals and other critters, categorized here as mammals, reptiles, amphibians, and arthropods, have been introduced to the island, and are not native. None of the deer, goats, cows, donkeys, cats, dogs, mongooses, or iguanas are indigenous. People brought them here as pets, for agricultural uses, or for pest control. Some of the animals that arrived by accident as stowaways or as domestic animals are now left to run wild. The list is numerous and diverse. This checklist includes a few of St. John's more commonly seen critters. *Photographs are included to aid with identification. For illustrative purposes, they include images taken locally as well as photographs taken elsewhere of critters of the same family and species.*

Fish Eating Bat, Susan Ellis, Courtesy Wikimedia under creative commons license, https://commons.wikimedia.org/wiki/File:Captive_Noctilio_leporinus.jpg

Bats *(Noctilo leparinus)*
The only mammal native to St. John is the bat. Some bat species are important pollinators and seed dispersal agents for many fruit-bearing trees and shrubs. They also consume vast quantities of insects, including mosquitoes. There are six species of bats that inhabit St. John: cave bats *(Brachyphylla cavernarum)*, a wide-nosed pollinator of trees; common house bats *(Molossus molossus)*; fish-eating bats *(Noctilio leporinus)*; fruit-eating bats *(Artibeus jamaicensis)*; insect-eating bats *(Tadarida brasiliensis)*; and red fig-eating bats *(Stenoderma rufum)*. Taino people believed bats were the reincarnated spirits of deceased ancestors.

Deer, White-tailed *(Odocoileus virginianus)*
Can be found in various places such as at Calabash Boom, Lameshur Bay, Reef Bay, and Fish Bay. Deer were brought to St. John by the Danes in 1792 as game for hunting. They thrived, and in 1937 a lot more deer were transported to the island as part of the Wildlife Restoration Act. These deer have no island predators except humans. Females weigh about 80 pounds and bucks reach about 100 pounds.

Donkey
Wander freely. Very common in East End and Coral Bay areas. (See *East End, Sightseeing, St. John's Donkeys, pp. 96-97,* for a more complete description of donkeys.)

White-tailed Deer, Jonathunder, Courtesy Wikimedia under GNU free documentation and creative commons licenses, https://commons.wikimedia.org/wiki/File:OdocoileusVirginianus2007-07-28fawn.JPG

Donkeys, Fred Hsu, Courtesy Wikipedia under GNU free documentation license, https://commons.wikimedia.org/wiki/File:Caneel_Bay_Free_Roaming_Wild_Donkeys.jpg

CHECKLIST/MAMMALS, REPTILES, AMPHIBIANS, ARTHROPODS

Dragonfly *(Macrodiplax batteata)* Brightly colored creatures. Dragonflies are predators, both in their aquatic larval stage, when they are known as nymphs or naiads, and as adults. Several years of their lives are spent as nymphs living in fresh water; the adults may be on the wing for just a few days or weeks. They are fast, agile fliers, sometimes migrating across oceans, and often live near water. They have a uniquely complex mode of reproduction involving indirect insemination, delayed fertilization, and sperm competition. Variety of species. Found in South America, southern United States, and the Caribbean Antilles.

Dragonfly, Eric Haley, Courtesy Wikimedia under creative commons license, https://commons.wikimedia.org/wiki/File:Macrodiplax_balteata.jpg

Frangipani Caterpillar *(Pseudosphinx tetrio)* Larva of the frangipani sphinx moth. Brightly colored centipede that feeds on the leaves of the poisonous wild frangipani *(Voacanga africana)* to which it has a built-up immunity. Would-be predators avoid this centipede for fear of ingesting the secondhand poison that accumulates in their system. Their bold colors alert predators to danger.

Caterpillar, Hans Hillewaert, Courtesy Wikimedia under creative commons license, https://commons.wikimedia.org/wiki/File:Pseudosphinx_tetrio.jpg

Goats *(Capra aegagrus)*
There are many recognized breeds of domestic goats. Goat breeds (especially dairy goats) are some of the oldest defined animal breeds for which breed standards and production records have been kept. Selective breeding of goats generally focuses on improving production of fiber, meat, dairy products, or goatskin. Breeds are generally classified based on their primary use, though there are several breeds which are considered dual- or multi-purpose. On St. John goats are frequently found wandering freely in groups.

Goats

Golden Orb *(Nephila clavipes)*
Nephila are noted for the impressive webs they weave. Nephila consists of numerous species found in warmer regions around the world. They are commonly called "golden silk orb-weavers" or "giant wood spiders." They are the most common group of builders of spiral wheel-shaped webs often found on St. John. Webs are constructed in a stereotyped fashion. A framework of non-sticky silk is built up before the spider adds a final spiral of silk covered in sticky droplets. (See *Hiking Trails, #5 Cinnamon Bay Loop Trail, pp. 124-125*.)

Golden Orb, Jose Jeevan and Rani, Courtesy Wikimedia under creative commons license, https://commons.wikimedia.org/wiki/File:Argiope_catenulata_at_Kadavoor.jpg

Puerto Rican Racer Snake *(Borkenophis portoricensis)*
Commonly called island racers. Occasionally spotted on St. John. Like all snakes in the Virgin Islands this snake is not poisonous.

Racer Snake, Yasmapuz & ace_heart, Courtesy Wikimedia under creative commons license, https://commons.wikimedia.org/wiki/File:Culebrita_completa.jpg

Hermit Crab, Daniel Kraft, Courtesy Wikimedia under creative commons license, https://commons.wikimedia.org/wiki/File:Hermite_Crab_Dry_Tortugas.jpg

Hermit Crab, Caribbean *(Coenobita clypeatus)*
Creepy, crawly little creature that doggedly hauls its shell-house around on its back. Heard tumbling down hillsides as they make their way to the seashore to mate and lay eggs. These land crabs burrow and hide under the roots of large trees and can often be found a considerable distance inland. They are both herbivores as well as scavengers. Females release fertilized eggs into the ocean. The spawning,-called "washing," occurs on certain nights, usually around August.

Iguana

Iguana *(Cyclura cornuta stejnegeri)*
Prehistoric looking greenish reptile often seen lounging in the sun or perched on tree branches. Generally mild-tempered, but have been known to bite if cornered. Best to stay clear. During mating season, they dig holes in hillsides to deposit their eggs and often bore false holes to distract predators from finding their eggs.

Lizard

Ground Lizard *(Ameiva exsul)*
Lizards are particularly helpful since they eat mosquitoes, which are plentiful in the evening. They can be seen scurrying up walls and tree trunks. Male ground lizards display a reddish pouch, or dewlap, to show territoriality; that combined with a series of "push-ups" warns off competing males and attracts females.

   Common to the island are the large scaly lizard, ground lizard, man lizard, snake lizard, and two Gecko species—the wood slave and the money lizard.

Millipede, Berit, Courtesy Wikimedia under creative commons license, https://commons.wikimedia.org/wiki/File:And_then_I_found_this_(6859016284).jpg

Millipede *(Diplopoda)*
Variations of this family are found worldwide. The species seen locally (similar to the one above) has a long black body and seemingly thousands of tiny legs. Some tropical varieties secrete a substance that can cause skin and eye irritations. Millipedes are a group of arthropods characterized by two pairs of jointed legs on most body segments. They are slow-moving and eat decaying leaves and other dead plant matter. Approximately 12,000 millipede species have been identified. (See *Hiking Trails, #5 Cinnamon Bay Loop Trail, p. 124.*)

Mongoose, Chung Bill Bill, Courtesy Wikimedia under creative commons license, https://commons.wikimedia.org/wiki/File:Small_asian_mongoose.jpg

Mongoose *(Herpertidae)*
Furry little rodent-like creatures seen scurrying across roads or down trails. Very shy. Small Indian mongoose was brought to St. John from India to rid the island of rats. The experiment failed, so now we have both! By the way, the plural of mongoose is "mongooses, " not "mongeese." The mongoose has no natural enemy on St. John. Often seen along the road at Lameshur Bay.

"No See-Um" Pesky nearly invisible little insects that ferociously attack your legs and feet at the beach. Particularly abundant after a rainfall when the beach sand is wet. Bite marks generally disappear quickly, but they are a genuine nuisance *(Sorry, no see-um, so no photo.)*

CHECKLIST/MAMMALS, REPTILES, AMPHIBIANS, ARTHROPODS

Scorpion

Scorpion *(Centruroides gracilis)*
Scorpions are predatory arachnids, easily recognized by a pair of grasping pedipalps and their narrow, segmented tail, often carried in a characteristic forward curve over the back, ending with a venomous stinger. There are 1,750 species of scorpions; only about 25 carry venom capable of killing a human. Those found in the Virgin Islands carry venom that's not much different from a bee sting in pain, sometimes accompanied by a numbing sensation. No treatment is normally required for adults; however, medical care should be sought for elderly people and young children.

Tarantula, George Chernilevsky, Courtesy Wikimedia, PD, https://commons.wikimedia.org/wiki/ File:Brachypelma_klaasi_2009_G01_cropped.jpg

Tarantula *(Brachypelma klaasi)*
Virgin Islands tarantulas live in holes that they dig in the ground where they lie and wait for lizards and other unsuspecting prey. Their venom can be painful, but not harmful to humans.

Toad, Puerto Rican Crested *(Peltophryne lemur)*
Frogs and toads found in the Virgin Islands include the Virgin Islands coqui, Cuban tree frog (an invasive species), giant neotropical toad, common coqui, red-eyed coqui, Whistling coqui, Puerto Rican crested toad *(pictured here)*, Hispaniolan ditch frog, and the yellow mottled coqui. Several of the frogs are in danger of extinction due to loss of habitat.

Puerto Rican Crested Toad, Jan P. Zegarra, U.S. Fish and Wildlife Service, Courtesy Wikipedia, PD, https://commons.wikimedia.org/wiki/ File:Puerto_Rican_crested_toad.jpg

Norwegian Rat *(Rattus norvegicus)*
Rats were mistakenly brought to the Virgin Islands by early colonial Europeans. Originally from Asia. They feed on pretty much anything, including plants, bird and reptile eggs, and any treats left carelessly scattered about. Besides Norwegian rats (often called brown rats), there are also the slightly smaller tree rats (frequently referred to as black rats, ship rats, and roof rats).

White Sulphur Butterfly *(Pieridae)*
A common butterfly found throughout the Virgin Islands. The *Pieridae* are a large family of butterflies. This family has about 76 genera and 1,100 species. The pigments that give the coloring to these butterflies are derived from waste products in the body. Butterflies were called "butter-coloured flies" by early British naturalists. They feed on the nectar of flowers and, moving from flower to flower, transfer pollen.

Norwegian Rat, *Anemore Projectors (talk), Courtesy Wikipedia under creative commons license,* https://commons.wikimedia.org/wiki/File:Rattus_norvegicus_-Fairlands_Valley_Park,_Stevenage,_England-8.jpg

White Sulphur, *Svdmolen, Courtesy Wikimedia under GNU free documentation and creative commons licenses,* https://commons.wikimedia.org/wiki/File:Anteos_clorinde-01_(xndr).jpg

Checklist of Birds

Throughout the year some 144 species of birds can be seen in the park. Of that number, about 35 are permanent residents. Others are either neotropical migrants or summer visitors. Neotropical migrants, like the shorebirds and warblers, visit from November to April. Summer seabirds are in residence from April to October. (The NPS publishes a comprehensive *Bird Checklist* for St. John. Inquire about availability at the visitor center in Cruz Bay.)

One of the best places to bird watch is from the Francis Bay Trail. As you walk along the dry forest trail you can see hummingbirds, flycatchers, doves, pigeons, cuckoos, and thrashers. The trail borders a salt pond, where there are ducks, stilts, moorhens, and migratory shorebirds. On the beach, you can spot pelicans and gulls. There are other salt ponds in dry, arid areas around the island, which are also good places to bird watch.

Our checklist includes a few of St. John's more commonly seen birds. *Photographs are included to aid with identification. For illustrative purposes, they include images taken locally as well as photographs taken elsewhere of birds of the same family and species as those living here. For further information on local birds, visit the Virgin Islands National Park website at https://www.nps.gov/viis.*

Bahama Duck, Putneymark, Courtesy Wikimedia under creative commons license, https://commons.wikimedia.org/wiki/File:Galapagos_white-cheeked_pintail_duck_-Santa_Cruz_highlands.jpg

Bahama Duck
(Anas bahamensis)
The only permanent resident duck. Easy to recognize by its red bill mark and white cheek. Natural habitat is a salt pond. Feeds on aquatic plants and small creatures caught by dabbling. They nest on the ground under vegetation and near water.

Bananaquit
(Coereba flaveola)
Also known as "sugar birds." Lively birds that eat a wide variety of foods including fruit and insects. Leave a small bowl of sugar water out to attract them. Natural habitat is the dry forest. Official bird of the Virgin Islands.

Bananaquit, Leon-Bojarczuk, Courtesy Wikimedia under creative commons license, https://commons.wikimedia.org/wiki/File:Bananaquits.jpg

Brown Pelican
(Pelecanus occidentalis)
The brown pelican is found throughout the Americas. They are a very gregarious bird that lives in flocks. Pelicans are exceptionally buoyant thanks to internal air sacks, which are located beneath the skin and in the bones. They are as graceful in the air as they are clumsy on land. When foraging, they dive bill-first, often submerging completely below the surface as they snap up their prey. Upon surfacing, they spill water from the throat pouch before swallowing their catch.

Brown Pelican, Terry Foote, Courtesy Wikimedia, licensed under creative commons, https://commons.wikimedia.org/wiki/File:Brown_Pelican21K.jpg

Brown-throated Conure
(Aratinga pertinax)
The brown-throated conure, also known as the brown-throated parakeet, was introduced to the Virgin Islands by being carried here by a visitor from Curacao. It feeds on fruits and seeds from various trees. Typically flies in a group and can be distinguished by its loud squawks. The bird is endemic to northern South America and can be found in Puerto Rico and the U.S. Virgin Islands.

Brown-throated Conure, Alexander Yates, Courtesy Wikimedia under creative commons license, https://commons.wikimedia.org/wiki/File:Aratinga_pertinax_-national_park_-Aruba-8.jpg

Cattle Egret *(Bubulcus ibis)*
A common species of heron found in the tropics, cattle egrets are easily recognized by their generous size and white plumage. They nest in colonies,

usually near bodies of water and often with other wading birds. Their nest is a platform of sticks in trees or shrubs. They often accompany cattle, catching insects attracted to these and other large animals. This benefits both species, but it also contributes to the spread of tick-borne animal diseases.

Grey Kingbird
(Tyrannus domincensis)
The grey kingbird is a passerine bird. It can be found in Florida, the Caribbean, Central America, and parts of South America. Grey kingbirds like to perch on exposed high tree limbs, occasionally sallying out to feed on insects, their staple diet. They aggressively defend their territory against intruders, including mammals and much larger birds.

Cattle Egret, Stuart Burns, England; Courtesy Wikimedia and Wikipedia under creative common license, https://commons.wikimedia.org/wiki/File:Bubulcus_ibis_-Gambia_-frog_in_beak-8.jpg

Kingbird, Charles J. Sharp, Courtesy Wikipedia under creative commons license, https://commons.wikimedia.org/wiki/File:Grey_kingbird_(Tyrannus_dominicensis_vorax).jpg

Hummingbird, Antillean Crested
(Orthorhyncus cristatus)
Abounds throughout the Virgin Islands and Puerto Rico. The male has green upper and black underside with a noticeable crest of green or blue; females and

Antillean Crested Hummingbird, Charles J. Sharp, Courtesy Wikipedia under creative commons license, https://commons.wikimedia.org/wiki/File:Antillean_crested_hummingbird.jpg

babies have less conspicuous crests, green upper and a white or grey underside with their forked tail feathers showing bits of white.

Hummingbird, Green-throated Carib *(Eulampis holosericeus)* Mostly green with a patch of purplish blue on its chest, black stomach, purple black tail, and slightly curved bill *(seen below)*. Male and female are alike. Natural habitat is the dry forest. Readily found throughout Puerto Rico and the Virgin Islands.

Kestrel *(Falcos sparvetius)* The American kestrel is the smallest and most common falcon in North America. It also ranges to South America and is a well-established species that has evolved seventeen subspecies adapted to different environments and habitats throughout the Americas. The kestrel usually hunts in energy-conserving fashion by perching and scanning the ground for prey to ambush, though it also hunts from the air. It sometimes hovers in the air

Green-throated Carib, Postdif, Courtesy Wikipedia under GNU Free documentaion and creative commons licenses, https://commons.wikimedia.org/wiki/File:Eulampis_jugularis_a1.jpg

with rapid wing beats while honing in on prey. Its diet typically consists of grasshoppers and other insects, lizards, mice, and small birds. Common to the Virgin Islands.

Kestrel, Greg Hume, Courtesy Wikipedia under creative commons license, https://commons.wikimedia.org/wiki/File:Female_American_Kestrel.jpg

Laughing Gull *(Larus atricilla)* This migratory gull found on St John from April to October is a seabird that uses St John's offshore cays to nest. Gulls are usually found feeding with pelicans, but can also be seen begging for food. The laughing gull's name was derived from its raucous call, which sounds like a high-pitched laugh, "ha…ha…ha…."

Pearly-eyed Thrasher
(Margarops fuscatus)
Brown upper body, white with brown below, and large white marks on tail. Extremely bold, prolific breeders found throughout the Caribbean. An opportunistic omnivore that feeds primarily on large insects, but also feeds on fruits and berries, and will occasionally eat lizards, frogs, small crabs, other birds' eggs, and nestlings.

Laughing Gull, Jersyko at England Wikipedia, Courtesy Wikimedia under GNU free documentation and creative common licenses, https://commons.wikimedia.org/w/index.php?curid=4491374

Smooth-billed Ani
(Crotophage ani)
Sometimes called the "black witch," this bird is surrounded by local superstition suggesting it is a harbinger of impeding death. Thankfully, there have been many reported encounters with this bird without any dire consequences. Found in Florida, the Bahamas, the Caribbean, and parts of Central and South America. The ani nest is built communally. Several females lay their chalky blue eggs in the nest, and then share incubation and feeding. It's a very gregarious species, always found in noisy groups. Feeds on lizards, frogs, termites, and large insects.

Pearly-eyed Thrasher, Dick Daniels, Courtesy Wikimedia under GNU free documentation and creative commons licenses, https://commons.wikimedia.org/wiki/File:Pearly-eyed_Thrasher_StJohn_RWD.jpg

Black Witch, Charles J. Sharp, Courtesy Wikipedia under creative commons license, https://commons.wikimedia.org/wiki/File:Smooth-billed_ani_(Crotophaga_ani)_GC.JPG

Zenaida Dove *(Zenaida aurita)*
A member of the bird family *Columbidae*, which includes doves and pigeons. It's the national bird of the Caribbean island of Anguilla, where it is erroneously called "turtle dove." These birds forage on the ground, eating grains and seeds, sometimes also insects. They often swallow fine gravel to assist with digestion and will also ingest salt from mineral rich soils or livestock salt licks.

Zenaida Dove, *Charles J. Sharp, Courtesy Wikipedia under creative common license, https://commons.wikimedia.org/wiki/File:Zenaida_dove_(Zenaida_aurita)_male.JPG*

Checklist of Corals, Fish, and Marine Life

Corals

A coral is a tiny animal (cnidarian) with tiny plants (zooxanthellae algae) living inside it. Coral takes calcium from seawater and uses it to build a limestone skeleton providing a home for algae, which in turn provides energy for the coral. Zooxanthellae algae also gives coral its color.

Many corals grow together to form colonies, which are the various and fantastic shapes you see. Coral colonies grow very slowly, sometimes only a few millimeters every year. Lots of colonies growing close together make up the growing structure of the coral reef. Stepping on or even brushing corals can kill them. The world's coral reefs have been steadily dying from bleaching and pollution, so it's critical to be mindful of the fragility of their existence.

Below are examples of some of the most common coral types found at shallow depths close to St. John's shoreline. *Photographs are included to aid with identification. For illustrative purposes, they include images of corals taken locally as well as photographs taken elsewhere of examples of the same family and species. For further information on various coral formations, visit the Virgin Islands National Park website at https://www.nps.gov/viis.*

Brain Coral
(Diptoria lebyrinthiformis)
Brain coral belongs to a group known as the stony corals. The stony corals comprise

Brain Coral, Jan Derik, Courtesy Wikimedia, released into PD, https://commons.wikimedia.org/wiki/File:Brain_coral.jpg

the basic building blocks of coral reefs. The brain coral derives its name from its brain-like appearance.

Elkhorn Coral *(Acropora palmata)* Like brain coral, branching and pillar corals also belong to the stony or hard coral group. Pillar corals grow upward in

Elkhorn Coral, *Paul Asman and Jill LeNoble, Courtesy Wikimedia under creative commons license, https://commons.wikimedia.org/wiki/File:Elkhorn_coral_Acropora_palmata_(2442957411).jpg*

Staghorn Coral, *Albert Kok, Courtesy Wikimedia under PD, https://commons.wikimedia.org/wiki/File:Hertshoon.jpg*

clusters of heavy cylindrical spires. Branching corals also grow upward, but their branches are flattened often resembling the familiar horns and antlers of animals such as elk and moose, after which some are named.

Staghorn Coral *(Aeropora cervicnis)* A pillar coral and member of the stony coral group. Easily identified by its stag-like "antlers."

Fire Coral
(Millepora)
Fire coral belongs to the hydrocoral group. Fire coral will produce a painful burning sensation when touched, so stay clear. They are often mistaken for stony coral. There are several group patterns, including blade coral, branching coral, and box fire coral. These corals can be readily identified by their smooth surface and generally tan to mustard color. Fire coral will frequently encrust or "splatter" themselves over other coral colonies.

Fire Coral, Nick Hobgood, Courtesy Wikimedia under creative commons license, https://commons.wikimedia.org/wiki/File:Millepora_alcicornis_(Branching_Fire_Coral).jpg

Ventalina, Sea Fan
(Gorgonia ventalina)
Bushy and feather-like corals that are part of the gorgonians or soft coral group because their skeletons have a flexible, non-rigid shape. Members of the group include sea fans, sea rods, sea whips, and sea plumes. Their tree-like limbs are not calcareous, but are instead composed of a soft rubber-like material. Only the skeletal spicules, often visible in the translucent limbs, are calcareous. Gorgonians come in a range of pastel colors and are usually found clinging to rocks, rubble, and reefs.

Sea Fan, Lauretta Burke, Courtesy Wikimedia under creative commons license, https://commons.wikimedia.org/wiki/File:Reef_247.jpg

Fish & Other Marine Life

Trying to identify a specific type of fish from the 400 species that inhabit the area can be a daunting task. Some of the wide variety of species include parrot, drum, damsel, angel, and butterfly fish. Below is a checklist of some of the more common fish and other marine life around St. John. *Photographs are included to aid with identification. For illustrative purposes, they include images of fish and marine life taken locally as well as photographs taken elsewhere of examples of the same family and species as those living here. For further information about local fish and marine life, visit the Virgin Islands National Park website at https://www.nps.gov/viis.*

Banded Butterflyfish
(Chaetodon striatus)
The banded butterflyfish is silver and white with two black bands on its body and another on its head, running from eye to eye. They are typically seen flitting about in pairs on reef tops.

Barracuda
(Sphyraena barracuda)
Frequently found in shallow waters. Barracuda like to hide under shadows of boats. Larger ones need to be avoided when swimming or diving from boats. Found close to reefs alone or in a small cluster.

They have a long silver body with random dark splotches or bands, a big underslung jaw, and sharp teeth. They are voracious predators and hunt using a classic lie-in-wait or ambush technique. Some species can be dangerous to swimmers.

Branded Butterflyfish, *Bernard E. Picton, Courtesy Wikimedia under GNU free documentation and creative commons licenses, https://commons.wikimedia.org/w/index.php?curid=1022484*

Barracuda, *Laban712, Courtesy Wikimedia under PD, https://commons.wikimedia.org/wiki/File:Barracuda_laban.jpg*

Blue Chromis
(Chromis cyanea)
Lives in shallow water. Often found on the surface of reefs feeding on plankton. Males maintain a solitary breeding territory. After breeding with multiple females, they guard the eggs until the planktonic larvae hatch.

Blue Tang
(Acanthurus coeruleus)
Lives in shallow water. Blue tangs are a type of doctorfish that range

Blue Chromis, Brian Gratwicke, Courtesy Wikimedia under creative commons license, https://commons.wikimedia.org/w/index.php?curid=46675483

from pale blue to dark blue to black with dark-blue peripheries. The coral pictured here is *Dendrogyra cylindrus* (pillar coral). Note the sea fan at the foot of the coral.

Four-eye Butterflyfish
(Chaetodon capistratus)
Found at the top of reefs, often with a partner. Silver grey body marked by thin, black lines. The species gets its name from a large, dark spot on the rear portion of each

Blue Tang, Scott Bair, Courtesy Wikimedia under creative commons license, https://commons.wikimedia.org/wiki/File:Acanthurus_coeruleus_(blue_tang)_(San_Salvador_Island,_Bahamas)_5_(15962615858).jpg

Four-eye Butterflyfish, Chris Huss, National Oceanic and Atmospheric Administration, Courtesy Wikipedia released into PD, https://en.wikipedia.org/wiki/Foureye_butterflyfish

side of the body. Most predators aim for the eyes, and this false eye spot may trick the predator into believing the false-eyed fish will flee tail first.

French Angelfish
(Pomacanthus paru)
French angelfish are common in shallow reefs, usually in pairs. During the day they are out and about but come night seek shelter in their designated hiding spots. This fish tastes good and is sold at fish markets. It feeds on sponges, algae, bryozoans, zoantharians, gorgonians, and tunicates. Spawning pairs are strongly territorial and usually both partners vigorously defend their territory against neighboring pairs.

French Angelfish, Albert Kok, Courtesy Wikimedia under GNU free documentation and creative commons licenses, https://commons.wikimedia.org/wiki/File:Pomacanthus_paru3.jpg

Grouper
(Epinephelus striatus)
Important to the commercial fishery in the West Indies, but endangered by overfishing. Lives in sea reefs. This solitary fish feeds in the daytime, mainly on other fish and small crustaceans such as crabs and small lobsters. Groupers spawn in December and January, always around the time of the full moon, when vast

Grouper, Bernard Dupont, Courtesy Wikimedia under creative commons license, https://commons.wikimedia.org/wiki/File:Nassau_Grouper_(Epinephelus_striatus)_(36644405756).jpg

numbers of grouper cluster together to mate in the moonlight. Historic spawning areas are easy targets for fishing, which tends to remove the reproductively active members of the group. The governments of the United States, Cayman Islands, and Bahamas have instituted closed fishing seasons for the grouper.

CHECKLIST/CORALS, FISH, MARINE LIFE   191

Hawksbill Turtle, B. Navez, Courtesy Wikimedia under GNU free documentation and creative commons licenses, https://commons.wikimedia.org/wiki/File:Eretmochelys_imbricata_01.jpg

Hawksbill Turtle *(Eretmochelys imbricate)*
There are seven species of sea turtles. Three of these inhabit the waters of St. John. The two most common are the green and hawksbill turtles *(pictured above)*. The third species, the leatherback, is rarely seen. A mature hawksbill weighs between 100 and 150 pounds and measures about 25 inches long. Female hawksbills return every two to three years to beaches where they were born to lay their eggs. They lay three to five nests per season with about 130 eggs each. The hawksbill has a distinctive and beautiful carapace. They were harvested almost to extinction for their shell, which was used to create jewelry, combs, and brushes. Their diet includes sponges, other invertebrates, and algae. They can be found along rocky ledges and coral reefs where they seek shelter. (See *Francis Bay, North Shore Tour, p. 81,* for photo of the green turtle.)

Lionfish, Michael Gobler, Courtesy Wikimedia under creative commons license, https://commons.wikimedia.org/wiki/File:Common_lion_fish_Pterois_volitans.jpg

Lionfish
(Pterois miles)
Highly invasive species. Lionfish can grow up to 9 inches per year, mature in less than 1 year, reproduce year-round, and lay 30,000 eggs every 4 days. Lionfish can eat prey up to 75% of their own body size; they have venomous spines and no natural predators in the Atlantic and Caribbean. Everyone is encouraged to report all sightings and kills to the CORE Foundation at *http://www.COREVI.org.* Tel: (340) 201-2342 or email *nolionfish@yahoo.com.*

Nurse Shark, Stevelaycock21, *Courtesy Wikimedia under creative commons license,* https://commons.wikimedia.org/wiki/File:Nurse_shark_turning.jpg

Nurse Shark
(Ginglymostoma cirratum)
Shark attacks are extremely rare in the Virgin Islands, but they do happen. Avoid waters being fished or where fish are being cleaned. Do not swim at night or at dusk or dawn. Remove shiny jewelry and do not enter the water if you are bleeding. Move out of the area or exit the water if a shark approaches too close or makes sudden movements or appears agitated.

Nurse sharks, the most common shark found around St. John, are found in tropical and subtropical waters of the Eastern and Western Atlantic and Caribbean. Often seen by snorkelers and divers, they are nocturnal and sleep under rock ledges or coral heads. The nurse shark is light yellowish-brown to dark-brown in color, sometimes with small, dark spots. It has a flattened body and a broad, rounded head with two conspicuous barbells between the nostrils, which are used to help find food. The mouth is filled with rows of serrated teeth for crushing hard-shelled prey.

Octopus
(Octopus briareus)
The Caribbean reef octopus has eight long arms that vary in length and diameter. Spotted at Frank Bay and other coral areas around St. John.

This species changes color and texture to blend in with its environment. It lives in rocky lairs that are difficult to locate. It is not a social animal, and it stays well away from other octopuses except for mating. It moves by sucking up water and expelling it quickly in a jet for propulsion. Ejects ink to escape predators.

Octopus, Alessandro Dona, *Courtesy Wikipedia under creative commons license,* https://en.wikipedia.org/w/index.php?curid=22170457

CHECKLIST/CORALS, FISH, MARINE LIFE 193

Parrot Fish
(Scarus taeniopterus)
A solitary fish named for their dentition, distinct from other fish. Their numerous teeth are arranged in a tightly-packed mosaic on the external surface of the jaw bones, forming a parrot-like beak with which they rasp algae from coral and other rocky substrates, which contributes to the process of bioerosion.

Parrot Fish, Laszlo ILYES, Courtesy Wikimedia under creative commons license, https://commons.wikimedia.org/wiki/File:Scarus_taeniopterus.jpg

Queen Angelfish
(Holacanthus ciliarus)
The adult queen angelfish overall body color can be described as blue to blue green with yellow rims on its scales. It's also known to have blue markings around each gill cover. Feeds on sponges, but also tunicates, jellyfish, and corals, as well as plankton and algae. Lives up to 15 years.

Queen Angelfish, Stan Shebs, Courtesy Wikimedia under GNU free documentation and creative commons licenses, https://commons.wikimedia.org/w/index.php?curid=563177

Reef Butterflyfish
(Chaetodon sedentarius)
The reef butterflyfish has a yellowish back and dorsal fin with silvery-white lower body and yellowish tail. They are usually seen in pairs along reefs and are wary of divers but can sometimes be approached very slowly for a photo.

Reef Butterflyfish, Bernard E. Picton, Courtesy Wikimedia under GNU free documentation and creative commons licenses, https://commons.wikimedia.org/w/index.php?curid=1022683

Sargeant Major
(Abudefduf saxatilis)
Likes all habitats, but mostly found in shallow water in loose groups. Great variation in colors, but most commonly with a yellow upper body and silver-grey below. Often has a yellow tinge near the back. Feeds on invertebrates, zooplankton, smaller fish, crustaceans, and various species of algae. Adult males have a more bluish coloration and less visible stripes.

Sargeant Major, Mathew T. Rader, Courtesy Wikimedia under CC BY-SA and creative commons licenses, https://commons.wikimedia.org/wiki/File:Sergeant_Major_fish_or_p%C3%ADntano_(Abudefduf_saxatilis)_a_species_of_damselfish_in_Curacao.jpg

Sharknose Goby
(Elacatinus evelynae)
Very small, torpedo-shaped fish. Black stripes run under the yellow ones from the snout, over the lower part of the eye to the end of the caudal fin. Feeds on ectoparasites found on other fish. Monogamous and are usually found in pairs. The one pictured here is resting on brain coral.

Sharknose Goby, Laszlo Ilyes, Courtesy Wikimedia under creative commons license, https://commons.wikimedia.org/w/index.php?curid=1718271

Smooth Trunkfish
(Lactoprys triqueter)
A species of boxfish that swims above reefs and over sandy areas. Found alone or sometimes in a small cluster. It has a dark-colored body spotted with white dots. The only one in its family that does not have a spine over the eye. Honeycomb pattern on mid-body. Mouth area, eyes, and base of pectoral fin are a solid dark color. It uses its protuberant lips to expel a jet of water, which disturbs the sandy seabed to find shallowly buried invertebrates.

Smooth Trunkfish, Becky Dayhill, U.S. National Oceanic and Atmospheric Administration, Courtesy Wikimedia, PD, https://commons.wikimedia.org/wiki/File:Lactophrys_triqueter_1.jpg

CHECKLIST/CORALS, FISH, MARINE LIFE   195

Southern Stingray
(Dasyatis americana)
This flattened diamond-shaped creature can be seen cruising in shallow waters with its nose buried in the sand looking for dinner or quietly resting while almost entirely covered in sand. The slender tail exposes a long serrated and venomous spine at the base, which is used for defense. Though not fatal to humans, their stinger can be very painful if stepped on.

Stingrays are nocturnal predators. They swim with a wave-like motion, making it easier for them to maneuver.

Southern Stingray, James St. John, Courtesy Wikimedia under creative commons license, https://commons.wikimedia.org/wiki/File:Dasyatis_americana_(southern_stingray)_(San_Salvador_Island,_Bahamas)_7_(16152781622).jpg

Spotfin Butterflyfish, Cholmes75, Courtesy Wikimedia under creative comms license, https://commons.wikimedia.org/wiki/File:Spotfin_butterflyfish.jpg

Spotfin Butterflyfish
(Chaetodon ocellatus)
The name is derived from the dark spot on the dorsal fin. This, combined with a vertical, black bar through the eye, is an adaptation that can confuse predators. The vertical black bar disappears as the fish gets older and other black lines become more prominent.

Spotted Drum
(Equetus punctatus)
Frequently observed during the day under ledges or near the opening of small caves. A nocturnal feeder, it leaves the protection of its daily shelter at night to feed mainly on small crustaceans.

Spotted Drum, Laszlo ILYES, Courtesy Wikimedia under creative commons license, https://commons.wikimedia.org/wiki/File:Equetus_punctatus_juvenile.jpg

Sea Urchin *(Paracentrotus lividus)*
Although most of St. John's underwater creatures are harmless, take care to swim clear of sea urchins. Their black thorns have arrow-like tips, painful if they become attached to your skin. The spines are difficult to extract. Lime juice is a local remedy used for dissolving spines.

Sea urchins move slowly, feeding mostly on algae. Sea otters, starfish, wolf eels, triggerfish and other predators hunt and feed on them. Their roe is a delicacy in many cuisines. The sea urchin is moved along by a water vascular system, which allows the urchin to pump water into and out of the feet and thus propel itself along. The lower half of the body contains a mouth.

Sea Urchin

Yellow Tail *(Ocyurus chrysurus)*
The yellow tail is an abundant species of snapper. Mostly found around coral reefs, but also in other habitats. It is a commercially important species and has been farmed successfully. Sought as a game fish by recreational anglers and is a popular species in public aquariums.

Yellow Tail, Transity, Courtesy Wikimedia under GNU free documentation and creative commons licenses, https://commons.wikimedia.org/wiki/File:2006-10-06_18_-_Yellow-tail_Snapper.JPG

Checklist of Trees, Plants, and Cacti

There over 750 flora species growing on St. John. Our checklist includes some of the more common flora. Plants and trees identified with **red typeface** are poisonous or can cause harm or infection and **contact should be avoided.** *Photographs are included for illustrative purposes. They include images of trees, plants, and cacti taken locally as well as photographs taken elsewhere.*

Various species are identified throughout our guidebook. Some of these are cross-referenced in our text and checklist, which also includes additional species not cited in the text. For further information about local flora, visit the Virgin Islands National Park website at *https://www.nps.gov/viis.* For a more extensive account of local plants and trees, visitors may also wish to purchase a copy of *Learning about Trees and Plants*, by Gail Karlsson with Suki Dickson Buchalter, Kevel Lindsay, and Eleanor Gibney. It's available in the online store of the Friends website at *https://www.friendsvinp.org.*

Common Trees

Banana
(Musa acuminate)
The banana is probably native to Malaysia. From there it spread to the Philippines and eventually South America and westward to Africa. It was introduced to nearby Hispaniola (Dominican Republic) in 1516. Only a few varieties are grown on St. John. The fig or lady finger banana is one of the most popular local bananas and can be

Fig Banana

distinguished by its small size. It has a heavy root system that makes it resistant to wind damage. It blooms during mid-summer, late summer, and early fall.

Bay Rum
(Pimenta racemosa)
A smooth-barked tree with dark-green, shiny, fragrant leaves that is native to the Caribbean. The tree's leaves are used medicinally, and their oil is used to make an aftershave cologne called "bay rum." Extraction of the oil from the leaves provided St. John with one of its most important industries. (See *Hiking Trails, #5 Cinnamon Bay Loop Trail, p. 120,* and *#22 Reef Bay Trail, p. 147.*) In addition to its use in aftershaves, soaps, and lotions, leaves are used in tea, sauces, stews, and preserves.

Baobab tree
(Adansonia digitata)
(Photo bottom of page.) These long-lived trees are typically found on the dry, hot savannas of sub-Saharan Africa, where they dominate the landscape and reveal the presence of a water source from afar. Their growth rate is determined by ground water or rainfall, and their maximum age, which is subject to much conjecture, seems to be in the order of 1,200 years. They have traditionally been valued as a source of food, water, health remedies, and places of shelter. (See *Hiking Trails, #21 L'Esperance Trail, pp. 142-145.*)

Bay Rum, David Stang, Courtesy Wikimedia under creative commons license, https://commons.wikimedia.org/wiki/File:Pimenta_racemosa_19zz.jpg

Baobob, Roburq, Courtesy Wikimedia under creative commons license, https://commons.wikimedia.org/wiki/File:Adansonia_digitata_-_baobabs.JPG

Breadfruit *(Artocarpus altillis)*
Large, green fruit found on tall, handsome trees *(pictured p. 199)*. Originally brought to the West Indies from Tahiti by Captain Bligh in 1793 as a food staple

and high-energy source for enslaved laborers. Easily propagated from cuttings. Today it is grown in some 90 countries throughout Southeast Asia, the Caribbean, Central America, and Africa. Its name is derived from the texture of its moderately ripe fruit when cooked; similar to freshly baked bread and having a potato-like flavor. The timber of breadfruit has been used for building boats and houses in the tropics. The leaves can be dried and made into a tea, which has been used as a remedy for high blood pressure and heart ailments.

Cacao
(Thopbroma cacao)

Breadfruit, Hans Hillewaert/CC BY-SA 4.0, Courtesy Wikimedia under creative commons license, https://en.wikipedia.org/wiki/Breadfruit

The cacao tree, whose fruit *(pictured below)* is used in the manufacture of chocolate, is native to the Amazon Basin. More than 4,000 years ago, it was consumed by pre-Columbian cultures along the Yucatán. Apparently when Moctezuma II dined, he took no other beverage than chocolate, served in a golden goblet. Flavored with vanilla or other spices, his chocolate was whipped into a froth that dissolved in the mouth. Chocolate was introduced to Europe and later the West Indies by the Spaniards, and it became a popular beverage by the middle of the 1600s. (See *Hiking Trails, #5 Cinnamon Bay Loop Trail, pp. 123-124.*)

Calabash
(Crescentia cujete)
Native to tropical America, this gourd-like fruit was used by early inhabitants to fashion bowls and cups. *(Picture p. 200.)* Handy for baking, food storage, and bailing out boats. Often polished and prized for its unique shapes, which are sometimes formed by tying ropes tightly around the fruit when it is growing. In African traditional dance music, a dried calabash is often used as a percussion instrument

Cacao, Keith Weller, USDA ARS, Courtesy Wikimedia released under creative commons license, PD, https://commons.wikimedia.org/wiki/File:Cacao-pod-k4636-14.jpg

Calabash, Hans Hillewaert/CC BY-SA 4.0, Courtesy Wikimedia under creative commons license, https://commons.wikimedia.org/wiki/File:Crescentia_cujete_(fruit_and_foilage).jpg

Casha, Stan Shebs, Courtesy Wikipedia under GNU free documentation and creative commons license, https://commons.wikimedia.org/wiki/File:Acacia_smallii_4.jpg

played by striking with the fingers, wrists, or objects to produce sounds.

Casha Tree
(Vachellia farnesiana)
Commonly known as "sweet acacia" or "needle bush." Found in drier areas along the coastline, adjacent to trails, or on hillsides. These trees can reach heights of 30 feet. The flowers are processed through distillation to produce a perfume, which has been described as having a "delicious scent" *(pictured middle of page)*.

Symptoms: Its sharp spines can cause deep puncture wounds, followed by redness, painful swelling, localized pain, and infection.

Coconut Palm, Franz Eugen Köhler, published 1897, Courtesy Wikimedia under creative commons license, https://commons.wikimedia.org/wiki/File:Cocos_nucifera_-_K%C3%B6hler%E2%80%93s_Medizinal-Pflanzen-187.jpg

Remedy: If infection develops seek medical attention.

Coconut Palm
(Cocos nucifera)
The coconut palm is a naturalized tree, probably first brought to St. John from other tropical areas around the 1500s. The juice of the nut is a favorite drink with locals. The name "coconut" comes from the old Portuguese and Spanish word "coco," meaning "head" or "skull," after the three indentations on the coconut shell that resemble facial features. Often

referred to as the "tree of life." It provides food, fuel, cosmetics, folk medicine, and building materials, among many other uses.

Flamboyant *(Delonix reglia)*
Native of Madagascar. A large tree noted for its fern-like leaves and showy display of brilliant, orange-red flowers, which appear during the months of June and July. In many tropical parts of the world it is grown as an ornamental tree. It is readily found in the Virgin Islands and is the national flower of St. Kitts and Nevis.

Flamboyant, Berthold Werner. Courtesy Wikimedia under creative commons license, PD, https://commons.wikimedia.org/wiki/File:Flamboyant_BW_2.jpg

Frangipani, Wild
(Voacanga africana)
A tropical evergreen tree with glossy, lanced-shaped foliage and clusters of fragrant white flowers. Grows in dry areas and is often de-leafed by moth caterpillars. Parts of the plant are considered mildly toxic. Numerous medicinal uses in Africa.

Symptoms: Sap can cause a rash.
Remedy: Usually goes away after a few weeks.

Genip
(Melicoccus bijugatus)
Grows on a large deciduous tree with blotchy bark and dark-green leaves. The clustered edible fruits are quarter-sized with green, leathery skin, a single seed, and tart, pulpy body. Genip leaves of the female tree are thought to act as a repellent for sandflies. The fruits of the tree *(pictured here)* are widely embraced locally for their succulent sweetness.

Wild Frangipani, Doug, Courtesy Wikimedia under creative commons license, https://commons.wikimedia.org/wiki/File:Plumeria_alba2709449426.jpg

Genip, Hans B.~commonswiki, Courtesy Wikimedia under creative commons license, PD, https://commons.wikimedia.org/wiki/File:Melicoccus_bijugatus.jpg

Hog Plum, Marco Schmidt, Courtesy Wikimedia under creative commons license, https://commons.wikimedia.org/wiki/File:Spondias_mombin_MS4005.JPG

Some people believe that a double seeded genip, if eaten by a woman, will cause her to give birth to twins! (See *Hiking Trails, #22 Reef Bay Trail, p. 149.*)

Hog Plum
(Spondias mombin)
A deciduous tree native to tropical America, including the West Indies.

Trees are readily populated from cuttings. They produce a small yellow fruit, the pulp of which is either eaten fresh or made into juice, concentrate, or jellies. On St. John, the fruit was often fed to livestock. If the green leaves were chewed, it was locally thought to help clear a person's throat of mucus. The bark when boiled in water and rubbed on legs was thought to relieve weariness.

Kapok, User:Velela, Courtesy Wikimedia under creative commons license, PD, https://commons.wikimedia.org/wiki/File:Kapok_tree-pod.jpg

Kapok
(Ceiba pentandra)
The kapok or silk cotton tree can be found along the Reef Bay Trail. Kapok trees thrive in the rainforest. They can be 200 feet tall with trunks as wide as 9 feet with huge, buttressing roots. The seed pods *(middle photo)* release fluffy, silky material used for stuffing mattress cushions and life jackets. Indigenous people carved canoes and drums from the trunk. (See *Hiking Trails, #22 Reef Bay Trail, pp. 148-149.*)

Lignum Vitae
(Guaiacum officinale)
Pictured is a flowering branch from

Lignum Vitae, Dinesh Valke, Courtesy Wikimedia under CC BY-SA and creative commons licenses, https://commons.wikimedia.org/wiki/File:-Guaiacum_officinale_(2477708305).jpg

CHECKLIST/TREES, PLANTS, CACTI   203

Lime (Key), Forest & Kim Starr, Courtesy Wikimedia under creative commons license, https://commons.wikimedia.org/wiki/File:Starr_080610-8303_Citrus_aurantiifolia.jpg

Maho, Forest & Kim Starr, Courtesy Wikimedia under creative commons license, https://commons.wikimedia.org/w/index.php?curid=6144249

Mammee Apple, Biusch, Courtesy Wikimedia under creative commons license, https://commons.wikimedia.org/wiki/File:Mamey_de_Cartagena_de_Indias.jpg

this tree that produces wood so dense that it sinks in water. The wood contains a resin that self-lubricates it's pulp. It was often used on ships for bearings and bushing blocks that had rotating shafts. Locally the wood was used to mark property boundaries and as fence posts and other applications where rotting might be a problem. If the bark of the tree was boiled in water and consumed, it was thought to be a local remedy for fish poisoning and also an energy booster.

Lime (Key)
(Citrus aurantifolia)
The key lime is also known as the Mexican lime, West Indian lime or bartender's lime. The fruit *(pictured top of page)* is yellow when ripe. Key lime usually has a more tart and bitter flavor than other limes. Perhaps most distinguished as an ingredient in the key lime pie. Leaves when boiled to make tea are thought to be soothing to the stomach. (See *Hiking Trails, #22 Reef Bay Trail, pp. 149-150.*)

Maho
(Thespesia populnea)
This coastal tree is characterized by large bell-shaped flowers *(middle of page)* that turn from pale-yellow to purple. It has heart-shaped leaves and green seed pods that turn brown. It was once a main source of baste fibers for the production of cordage.

Mammee Apple
(Mammee Americana)
Mammee Americana, commonly known as mammee apple, tropical apricot, or South American apricot, is an evergreen tree, whose fruit is edible. The flower is fra-

grant, has 4 or 6 white petals, and reaches 1.6 inches wide when fully blossomed. The fruit is round or slightly irregular, with a brown or grey-brown, thick rind. The flesh is orange or yellow and can have various textures (crispy or juicy, firm or tender). Generally, the flesh smell is pleasant and appetizing. Under ripe fruits are rich in pectin, and the tree bark is high in tannin. (See *Hiking Trails, #5 Cinnamon Bay Loop Trail, p. 123.*)

Manchineel, Hans Hillewaert, Courtesy Wikimedia under creative commons license, https://commons.wikimedia.org/wiki/File:Hippomane_mancinella_(fruit).jpg

Manchineel *(Hippomane mancinella)*
Very poisonous tree with shiny, oval leaves. It can grow to 40 feet in height and bears small, highly toxic, green fruits that look like crab apples. In 1970, a member of the Danish gymnastic team visiting St. John took a bite of manchineel apple out of curiosity, which almost proved fatal.

Symptoms: Severe burning and blistering of the skin, temporary blindness. Remedy: Wash with soap and water, if severe reaction, seek medical help. (See *Annaberg School, North Shore Tour, p. 73-75.*)

Mango, Author, unknown. Courtesy Wikimedia under creative commons license, https://commons.wikimedia.org/wiki/File:Magnifera_indica.jpg

Mango *(Magifera indica)*
The mango *(middle of page)* is native to India and is a species of flowering plant in the sumac and poison ivy family. It bears one of the finest tropical fruits. Mango trees can be converted to lumber once their fruit-bearing lifespan has finished. The wood is used for musical instruments (such as ukuleles) and in the manufacture of low-cost furniture.

The fruit can be made into a preserve. As a bush remedy, the leaves are often made into a tea to treat rheumatism. (See *Hiking Trails, #5 Cinnamon Bay Loop Trail, p. 124.*)

Mangrove, Tau'olunga, Courtesy Wikimedia under GNU free documentation and creative commons licenses, https://upload.wikimedia.org/wikipedia/commons/f/f3/Rhizophora_mangle.jpg

Mangrove

Mangroves *(pictured p. 204)* are common along St. John's shoreline and inland. Red mangroves play an important role in protecting the shoreline from erosion. "Seeds" become fully mature plants before dropping off the parent tree. They are dispersed by water until eventually becoming embedded in the shallows. The red mangrove grows on aerial prop roots, which arch above the water level, giving stands of this tree the characteristic "mangrove" appearance. Mangroves provide nesting and hunting habitat for a diverse array of organisms.

Noni, Wilfredor, Courtesy Wikimedia under creative commons license, PD, https://commons.wikimedia.org/wiki/File:Noni_fruit_(Morinda_citrifolia).jpg

Noni or Painkiller *(Morinda citrifolia)*

Whitish-yellow fruit in the coffee family. Leaves are noted for their healing properties. For treatment of swollen areas, the leaves are crushed and heated using lard. It is a staple food among some cultures, and has been used in traditional medicine.

Papaya

(Carica papaya)
Native to the West Indies. Yields very tasty fruit. Papaya plants grow in three sexes: male, female, and hermaphrodite. The female will produce small inedible fruits unless pollinated. The hermaphrodite can self-pollinate. In some parts of the world, papaya leaves are made

Papaya, Franz Eugen Kohler, circa 1897, Courtesy Wikimedia under creative commons licence, PD, https://commons.wikimedia.org/wiki/File:Carica_papaya_-_K%C3%B6hler%E2%80%93s_Medizinal-Pflanzen-029.jpg

into tea as a treatment for malaria. Leaves are also used as a meat tenderizer. The seeds of the papaya are boiled in water and used as a remedy for treating diabetes.

Pap Vine, PumpkinSky, Courtesy Wikimedia under creative commons license, https://commons.wikimedia.org/wiki/File:Passion_Vine_NBG_LR.jpg

Pap Vine
(Passiflora maliformis)
The vine *(pictured p. 205)* produces a small fruit with purple, yellow, or green skin and a greyed-yellow to orange pulp that is aromatically-scented and flavored. It is usually eaten fresh or used to flavor drinks. The plant has long been thought to possess mystical qualities given its association with the crucifixion of Christ. The plant has been used as a remedy for calming nervous disorders.

Rue, Plenuska, Courtesy Wikimedia under reactive commons license, https://commons.wikimedia.org/wiki/File:Die_Weinraute,_lat._Ruta_graveolens,_Pflanze_mit_den_gelben_Bl%C3%BCten.jpg

Rue *(Ruta graveolens)*
Rue *(picture left)* is grown as an ornamental plant and herb. It is also cultivated as a medicinal herb, condiment, and, to a lesser extent, as an insect repellent. The herb is considered by some to be an antidote to poison. Ancients highly regarded the plant for its mystical powers, and some believed it offered protection against witchcraft. Locally it was used as a remedy for hysteria, unstable nerves, and eye ailments.

Sandbox

Sandbox
(Hura crepitans)
Commonly referred to as "Monkey No Climb" trees. Identifiable by bark, covered with dense, sharp thorns. The sandbox tree produces miniature pumpkin-shaped seed pods. When the pods of the large seed have ripened, they explode with a sound that mimics a gunshot. Found along the Reef Bay Trail and Annaberg and elsewhere.

Seagrape *(Cocoloba uvifera)*
This familiar shoreline tree is easy to identify by its round, leathery leaves. It bears

Seagrape, Forest & Kim Starr, Courtesy Wikimedia under creative commons license, https://commons.wikimedia.org/wiki/File:Starr_080604-6302_Coccoloba_uvifera.jpg

CHECKLIST/TREES, PLANTS, CACTI   207

Soursop, Damien Broilley, Courtesy Wikipedia and Wikimedia under creative commons license, https://commons.wikimedia.org/wiki/File:Annona_muricata_1.jpg

Sugar Apple, Muhammad Mahdi Karim, Courtesy Wikimedia under GNU free documentation license, https://en.wikipedia.org/wiki/Annona_squamosa

Sugar Apple *(Annona squamosa)*
Sugar-apple is a high energy source. It has lots of vitamin C and manganese and is a good source of thiamine and vitamin B. It also provides iron, phosphorus, and potassium in fair quantities.

clusters of green, ripening to purple, edible grapes. It serves as a dune stabilizer and protective habitat for small animals. The sap has been used for dyeing and tanning leather. The wood has occasionally been used in making furniture, as firewood, or for making charcoal. The fruit of the sea grape may be eaten raw, cooked into jellies and jams, or fermented into sea grape wine.

Soursop *(Annona muricata)*
This broadleaved, flowering evergreen produces a popular fruit whose flavor has been described as a combination of strawberry and pineapple, with sour citrus flavor notes, contrasting with an underlying creamy texture reminiscent of coconut or banana. The pulp is used to make fruit nectar, smoothies, fruit juice drinks, as well as candies, sorbets, and ice cream flavorings. The leaves boiled as a tea are widely promoted as having cancer curing properties. The tea is also consumed as a sedative to induce sleep.

Tamarind, B. Navez, Courtesy Wikimedia under GNU free documentation and creative commons licenses, https://commons.wikimedia.org/wiki/File:Tamarindus_indica_pods.JPG

Tyre Palm, BotBln, Courtesy Wikimedia under GNU free documentation and creative commons licenses, https://commons.wikimedia.org/wiki/File:Coccothrinax_alata_BotGard-Bln0712201B.JPG

Turpentine

West Indian Locust

Tamarind

(Tamarindus indica) The tamarind tree *(pictured p. 207)* produces brown, pod-like fruits that contain a sweet, tangy pulp, which is used in cuisines around the world. Large trees with feathery leaves often found along roadways and trails. The fruit can be used to make candies and juices or eaten raw. It is a tasty ingredient in Worcestershire sauce.

Tyre Palm *(Coccothrinax alta)*

The tyre palm is native to Puerto Rico and the Virgin Islands. It is commonly referred to as a "fan palm." Flowers are light yellow, and fruit is purple-black when ripe. It is the only remaining native palm on St. John. Used in traditional basketry, fish traps, brooms, and roof thatching. They also make attractive ornamental plants. (See *Hiking Trails, #5 Cinnamon Bay Loop Trail, p. 119*.)

Turpentine

(Bursera simaruba) It is often comically referred to as the "tourist tree" because the tree's bark is red and peeling, like the skin of sunburnt tourists. The tree yields ripe fruit year-round. The turpentine tree is also considered one of the more wind-tolerant trees. They are often planted to serve as wind protection for crops or as living fence posts, and if simply stuck into good soil, small branches will readily root and grow into sizable trees.

CHECKLIST/TREES, PLANTS, CACTI   **209**

The leaves and sap smell like turpentine. Locally, the leaves and bark were once used as a remedy for sore backs.

West Indian Locust *(Hymenaea courbaril)*
A common tree *(pictured p. 208)* in the Caribbean, South America, and Central America. It is a hardwood used for flooring, furniture, and decoration. Its fruit was a major food source for indigenous peoples. It can be eaten raw or dried and transformed into a powder used in cookies and soups. It is also an excellent concentrated feed for animals. (See *Hiking Trails, #22 Reef Bay Trail, p. 148*.)

Woman's Tongue, Forest & Kim Starr, Courtesy Wikimedia under creative commons license, https://commons.wikimedia.org/w/index.php?curid=6148197

Woman's Tongue
(Albizia lebbeck)
Takes its name from its seed pods, which, when rattling in the wind, apparently conjured up the playful association. On St. John, the tree grows well in windy, salty areas like around salt ponds.

Bougainvillea

Flowering Plants

Bougainvillea
(Bougainvillea)
This colorful plant grows as a woody vine or shrub, reaching 15 to 40 feet with heart-shaped leaves and

thorny stems. Its small flowers are generally white and inconspicuous, highlighted by several brightly colored, modified leaves, which are called bracts. The bracts can vary in color, ranging from white, red, mauve, purple, or orange. The fruit is a small, inconspicuous, dry, elongated achene, which has been reported to have anti-inflammatory, anti-bacterial, anti-viral, anti-tumor, and anti-fertility properties. The plant is also widely grown as an ornamental.

Century Plants *(Agave Americana)*
The name "century plant" refers to the long time the plant takes to flower. The number of years before yellow flowers occur depends on the vigor of the individual plant, the richness of the soil, and the climate. Tall plants that can grow 20 feet or more. On St. John this plant seems to flower after 10 years, not 100! Century plants were once commonly used locally as the traditional Christmas tree.

Century Plant

Ginger Thomas *(Tecoma stans)*
Flowering perennial shrub that produces the official flower of the Virgin Islands. It has sharply toothed, green leaves and

Ginger Thomas, M3847, Courtesy Wikimedia under GNU free documentation and creative commons licenses, https://commons.wikimedia.org/wiki/File:Yellow_elder.jpg

bears showy, golden-yellow, trumpet-shaped flowers. The flowers attract bees, butterflies, and hummingbirds. The plant produces pods containing yellow seeds with papery wings. Used as a bush reme-

Hibiscus, Photo by Eric Kounce TexasRaiser, Courtesy Wikimedia under creative commons license, https://commons.wikimedia.org/wiki/File:Hibiscus_Syriacus.JPG

Jasmine

dy for the treatment of jaundice, headaches, diabetes, fevers, and colds.

Hibiscus *(Hibiscus syriacus)*
Hibiscus, also called "rose of Sharon," is a species of flowering plant found growing throughout the Caribbean. *(Pictured p. 210.)* Typically seen as a red, trumpet-shaped flower, but can be found in many other colors and varieties.

Jasmine *(Jasminium)*
Jasmines are widely cultivated for the characteristic fragrance of their flowers. Dark-green, shiny leaves that are 3-6 inches long. Produces white, delicate, fragrant blooms that open at night. The flowers appear in clusters on bushes from late spring to summer.

Orleander

Oleander *(Nerium oleander)*
Oleander is one of the most poisonous, commonly grown, garden plants. Caterpillars of the polka-dot wasp moth feed primarily on oleander and survive by carefully eating only the pulp surrounding the leaf veins, avoiding the fibers. Oleander is a vigorous grower that is extensively used as an ornamental plant along roadsides and in private gardens.

Symptom: Vomiting, lightheaded, and heart blockage.
Remedy: If ingested seek medical attention immediately.

Aloe Vera

Anthurium, Kraysztof Ziarnek, Kenraiz, Courtesy Wikimedia and Wikipedia under creative commons license, https://commons.wikimedia.org/wiki/File:Anthurium_acaule_kz2.jpg

Thorny, Spiny Cactus, and other Plants

Aloe Vera
(Aloe barbadensis)
Aloe vera is widely grown as an ornamental plant *(pictured p. 211).* The species is popular with modern gardeners as a medicinal plant for a variety of ailments and for its interesting flowers, form, and succulence. This species survives in areas of low natural rainfall, making it ideal for low-water-use gardens.

Anthurium *(Anthurium acaule)*
There are over 500 varieties of these plants. Anthuriums are perennials that grow on the ground or in trees. The *Anthurium acaule* can be found in abundance along the Reef Bay Trail as can the *Anthurium cordatum* with its beautiful, heart-shaped leaves. Both varieties have green, snake-like pistols.

Catch & Keep *(Acacia retusa)*
A common weed that forms dense thickets of vine-like vegetation. Covered in hundreds of hooked spines, catch and keep is aptly named for its ability to hook into and hold anything. Grows profusely along the Brown Bay and Johnny Horn trails.

Symptoms: Barbed spines can penetrate skin causing dozens of cuts, irritation, redness, swelling, and infection.
Remedy: Wash wounds, apply antibiotic ointment or cream.

Catch & Keep

Christmas Bush, *Xemenendura, Courtesy Wikimedia under creative commons license, https://commons.wikimedia.org/wiki/File:Comocladia_dodonaea_1.JPG*

CHECKLIST/TREES, PLANTS, CACTI   213

Christmas Bush
(Comocladia dodonaea)
The sap of the plant and surface of the leaves contains urushiol poison, which is similar to the poison found in poison ivy. On St. John it is commonly seen in open canopies and along trails. It has dark-green leaves with a reddish hue. Looks like holly. *(Pictured p. 212.)*

Symptoms: Burning, itching skin, swelling, irritation, and rash that can last up to several weeks.
Remedy: Possible use of anti-itch creams or ointments.

Congo Root, Toluay, Courtesy Wikimedia, PD, https://commons.wikimedia.org/wiki/File:Petiveria._Guin%C3%A9..JPG

Congo Root *(Petriveria alliacea)*
Otherwise known locally as "strong man root." Used in a bath as a medicinal plant for the treatment of stomach and other aches. Also used as a cleaning agent for wood floors. It is a deeply-rooted, perennial shrub growing to 3 feet in height and has small, greenish flowers. The roots and leaves have a strong acrid, garlic-like odor, which taints the milk and meat of animals that graze on it.

Jimson Weed, Flobbado, Courtesy Wikimedia under creative common liscense, https://commons.wikimedia.org/wiki/File:Datura_innoxia_Mill._flower,_buds_and_foliage.jpg

Jimson Weed, Prickly Burr, or Deadly Nightshade
(Datura inoxia)
Extremely toxic member of the Belladonna family. The Aztecs used the plant as poultices for wounds. Many Native Americans used it as an entheogen for hallucinations and rites of passage. The small shrub is often found in recently disturbed areas such as

Jumbie Bean, Scott Zona, Courtesy Wikimedia under creative commons license, https://commons.wikimedia.org/wiki/File:Abrus_precatorius_—_Scott_Zona_001.jpg

Love Leaf

roadsides and should be avoided. Easily recognized by its trumpet-shaped flowers.

Symptoms: Delirium, increased heart rate, rapid breathing, amnesia, and even death.
Remedy: Seek immediate medical attention.

Jumbie Bean
(Abrus precatorius)
A herbaceous flowering plant *(pictured p. 213)* in the bean family. A slender, perennial climber with long, pinnate-leafleted leaves that twines around trees, shrubs, and hedges. The plant is best known for its seeds, which are used as beads and in percussion instruments, and which are toxic because of the presence of abrin. Ingestion of a single seed, well chewed, can be fatal to both adults and children.

Milk Bush

Symptoms: Nausea, vomiting, convulsions, liver failure, death.
Remedy: If ingested seek medical attention immediately.

Love Leaf (Clapper Bush)
(Bryophyllum pinnatum)
Love leaf is a succulent plant that is distinctive for the profusion of miniature plantlets that form on the margins of its phylloclades. Used as a remedy for kidney issues and high blood pressure. Legend has it that if you carve your name on a leaf along with the name of your girlfriend or boyfriend and the leaf takes root, it is a sure sign the object of your affections loves you too.

Milk Bush *(Euphorbia lactea)*
Extremely toxic. A small shrub-like tree used as an ornamental plant. Distinguished by hundreds of green, pencil-thin, cylindrical branches, it secretes a milky sap when cut or damaged.

Pipe Organ

Symptoms: Skin irritation, severe rash, and blisters; blindness if it gets in the eyes.

CHECKLIST/TREES, PLANTS, CACTI   **215**

Prickly Pear, David J. Stang, Courtesy Wikimedia under creative commons license, https://commons.wikimedia.org/wiki/File:Opuntia_repens_9zz.jpg

Remedy: Wash affected area immediately with soap and water. Seek immediate medical attention for eye or mouth exposure.

Pipe Organ/ Dildo Cactus
(Pilosocereus royenii)
A species of cactus readily found in Puerto Rico and the Virgin Islands. *(Pictured p. 214.)* Common names include Royen's tree cactus, dildo cactus, and pipe organ cactus. It is composed of multiple long, tubular-shaped branches, each ribbed with many sections and sharp spines. Often stretching 10-25 feet tall, the cactus has a thick skin with prickly needles. The meat of the cactus is used in some local food dishes.

Prickly Pear *(Opunita repens)*
The prickly pear is a species of cactus that is native to dry forests in Puerto Rico and the Virgin Islands. It is a small shrub with yellow flowers and red fruit. Spines easily penetrate cloth-

Sugar Cane

Sweet Lime, Kybrdgal, Courtesy Wikimedia under GNU free documentation license, https://commons.wikimedia.org/wiki/File:Triphasia_trifoliata_fruits.jpg

ing and can become imbedded in skin, with harmful effects.

Symptoms: Localized pain, inflammation, irritation, and rash.
Remedy: Remove spines carefully to alleviate pain.

Sugar Cane
(Saccharum officinarum)
A large and strong-growing species of grass. Its stout stalks are rich in sucrose. It arrived in the New World with Spanish explor-

Turk's Cap, Bordy Nathalie, Courtesy Wikimedia under creatve commons license, https://commons.wikimedia.org/wiki/File:Melocactus-intortus.jpg

ers and is now cultivated in tropical and subtropical countries worldwide for the production of sugar, ethanol, and other products. West Indian natural brown sugar is considered superior to refined white sugar in flavor, color, and nutritional values. (See *Hiking Trails, #9 Annaberg, pp. 129-130.*)

Sweet Lime *(Triphasia trifolia)*
Sweet Lime *(pictured p. 215)* is grown for its edible fruit. It has also been noted as a potential invasive in the Caribbean. It has gained some popularity as a bonsai plant. The sticky fruit was once used locally to seal letters and was also used as a preserve. (See *Hiking Trails, #5 Cinnamon Bay Loop Trail, p.126.*)

Turk's Cap Cactus
(Melocactus intortus)
Mature plants are easily recognizable by their cephalium, a bristle-coated structure at the apex of the plant, containing a mass of areoles from which small flowers grow. Since the red, wool-coated cephalium of the plant is

Wondering Jew, Mokkie, Courtesy Wikimedia under creative commons license, https://commons.wikimedia.org/wiki/File:Silvery_Wandering_Jew_(Tradescantia_zebrina)_5.jpg

CHECKLIST/TREES, PLANTS, CACTI **217**

Wild Maran

similar to the fez hat worn by Turkish male citizens during late Ottoman Empire, the plant is so named. The fruits of the cactus are pink and resemble the shape of pepper fruits. They are edible, and in the wild they are frequently dispersed by lizards and birds.

Wandering Jew
(Tradescantia zebrina)
It is commonly available and used as a houseplant and groundcover. *(Pictured p. 216.)* Tends to become an invasive species if not properly maintained. Its leaves have been used as a tea to treat high blood pressure.

Wild Maran *(Croton punctatus)*
Found in abundance in drier areas like around Salt Pond Bay. Once came in quite handy for a variety of household uses. The rough leaves were used for washing dishes and scrubbing pots and pans. Also used for sweeping out outdoor ovens. Apparently successful at keeping lice away as well.

Wild Pineapple
(Bromelia pinguin)
This species is native to Central America, Mexico, and West Indies. Features long, green leaves that look something like a pineapple. During Danish times, planters used to grow pinguin around the windows of their estate houses to keep prowlers away. It is commonly planted as a fence around pasture lands, on account of its prickly leaves. The fruit, known as "piñuela," is dug out, protective "hair" removed, then peeled like a banana and eaten. The plant can also be stripped of its pulp, soaked in water, and beaten with a wooden mallet to yield a fiber thread. The plant's sharp, thorny surface can hurt.

Wild Pineapple

Symptoms: Scratches, cuts, and shallow puncture wounds.
Remedy: Wash wounds, apply antibiotic ointment or cream.

Sources and Credits

Bibliography

"A Visit to the Bethany Moravian and the Nazareth Lutheran Churches," *by* Robin Swank, *Five Quarters, Selected Readings from the Archives of the St. John Historical Society,* 2010

Annaberg Sugar Mill, National Park Service, Publication date unknown

"Beachcombing in the Virgin Islands," by Paul Brooks, *Harper's Magazine,* December 1960 Issue, all rights reserved by *Harper's Magazine*

"Black History Spotlight: Julius E. Sprauve," February 14, 2008, staff, *The St. Thomas Source, "U.S. Virgin Islands," https://stthomassource.com/content/2008/02/14/black-history-spotlight-julius-e-sprauve/*

"Carl Emanuel Francis: From Cattle Dealer to Councilman," by Andrea Milam, February 11, 2007, *St. John Tradewinds, https://stjohntradewinds.com/carl-emanuel-francis-from-cattle-dealer-to-councilman/*

Countess Daisy, Arne Handberg Jakobsen, A. Handberg, 2019

Creoles & Continentals, Reflections on 300 Years of Colonial Life on St. John, by David Knight, Sr., online version, publication date unknown

"Digging Up Discoveries @Cinnamon Bay," by Andrea Milam, *St. John Magazine,* Issue No. 5, 2009

Danish National Archives Website, *https://www.sa.dk/ao-soegesider/en/collection/theme/8*

"Educator, Author and Community Activist Jadan Dies," staff, *The St. Thomas Source,* July 29, 2020 *https://stthomassource.com/content/2004/12/21/educator-author-and-community-activist-jadan-dies/*

"Enighed Estate House," by Andrea Milan, *St. John Magazine,* Issue No. 4, 2010

"Estate Cathrineberg & Jochumsdahl," by David W. Knight, *Five Quarters, Selected Readings from the Archives of the St. John Historical Society,* 2010

"Ethel McCully, Saved Virgin Islands Home from Condemnation," *New York*

220 STJ ON FOOT AND BY CAR

Times, January 4, 1981, Section 1

"Finding Out Different," by Nancy Flagg Gibney, *Five Quarters, Journal of the St. John Historical Society,* Vol III, Issue 3, November 2015

Grandma Raised the Roof, Ethel McCully, Crowell, 1954

A Guide to the Natural History of St. John, Doris Jadan, St. Thomas Graphic, 1985

"Guy Benjamin Dies at Age 98," staff, June 20, 2012, *The St. Thomas Source* U.S. Virgin Islands, *https://stthomassource.com/content/2012/06/20/guy-benjamin-dies-age-98/*

Herbs and Proverbs, Arona Petersen, A. Petersen, 1964

"Historic Cruz Bay Free-Colored Cemetery Restoration Taking Place," by Andrea Milam, special contributor, April 24, 2014, *News of St. John*

"Historical Perspective," by Chuck Pishko, *St. John Magazine,* Issue Fall/Winter, 2007

Kammerherreinden, A Story about Noble Ladies and Dead Libertines, ikke udgivet, Jens Ole Ravn-Nielsen, publication date to be determined

Leaflets from the Danish West Indies, C. E. Taylor, London, 1888

Learning About Trees and Plants, Gail Karlsson with Suki Dickson Buchalter, Kevel Lindsay and Eleanor Gibney, Zehngut Design, 2016

Me and My Beloved Virgin, Guy Benjamin, Benjamin's Pub. Co., 1981

My Island Kitchen, Erva Boulon, Virgin Islands Printing Company, 1965

National Register of Historic Places, Cruz Bay Town, Reference # 16000699, 2016, *https://www.nps.gov/nr/feature/places/pdfs/16000699.pdf)*

Night of the Silent Drums, John Lorenzo Anderson, Mapes Monde Editore, 1992

"Organic Farming," by Andrea Milam, *St. John Magazine,* Issue Fall/Winter, 2008

Profiles of Outstanding Virgin Islanders, Ruth Moolenarr, Virgin Islands Commission, DOE, Government of the Virgin Islands, 1972-1992
Report on the Execrable Conspiracy Carried Out by the Amina Negroes on

SOURCES AND CREDITS **221**

Danish Island of St. Jan in America 1733 by Pierre J. Pannet with Introduction by Aimery P. Caron and Arnold R. Highfield, translated and edited by Aimery P. Caron and Arnold R. Highfield, Antilles Press, Christiansted, St. Croix, USVI, 1984

Smiling Lizard Research at *http://www.smilinglizard.com*

St. John Backtime: Eyewitness Accounts from 1718 to 1956, Rafael Valls and Ruth Hull Low, Eden Hill Press, 1991

"St. John Mourns Miss Lucy, World Famous Taxi Driver and Restaurant Owner," October 3, 2007, staff, *The St. Thomas Source, https://stthomassource.com/content/2007/10/03/st-john-mourns-miss-lucy-world-famous-taxi-driver-and-restaurateu/*

"Senator Theovald Moorehead's Letter Brings Back Memories," *Wha's Happ'nin,'* Sis Frank, *https://stjohntradewinds.com/whas-happnin-by-sis-frank-19/*

St. John Voices: A Documentary Anthology of Daily Life on St. John 1718-1956, Ruth Hull Low, Eden Hill Press, 2010

"The Annaberg School at Mary's Creek," by David W. Knight, *Five Quarters, Selected Readings from the Archives of the St. John Historical Society,* 2010

The Danish West Indies Under Company Rule, 1671-1754 by Waldemar Westergaard, The Macmillan Company, 1917, Courtesy Internet Archive free library, *https://archive.org/stream/danishwestindies00west/danishwestindies00west_djvu.txt*

The Danish Colonization of St. John 1718-1733, Leif Calundann Larsen, Institute for History, Copenhagen University, 1980

"The Establishment of the East End Community of St. John," by David W. Knight, *Five Quarters, Selected Readings from the Archives of the St. John Historical Society,* 2010

"The Evolution of the Mocko Jumbie in the V.I.," *The St. John Source*, staff, March 1, 2019, *https://stjohnsource.com/2019/03/01/the-evolution-of-the-mocko-jumbie-in-the-v-i/)*

The French Intervention in the St. John Slave Revolt, 1733-34 Aimery P. Caron and Arnold R. Highfield, Bureau of Libraries, Museums, and Archaeological Services, Dept. of Conservation and Cultural Affairs, Charlotte Amalie, St. Thomas, V.I., 1981

222 STJ ON FOOT AND BY CAR

The Last Trail Bandit Guide to the Hiking Trails of St. John, Bob Garrison, 2014

"The Legend of Easter Rock," April 11, 2020, *News of St. John*

The Virgin Islands of the United States of America, Luther K. Zabriskie, G.P. Putnam's Sons, 1918

Trail Guide for Safe Hiking, National Park Service, publication date and printing source unknown

Understanding Annaberg, David W. Knight Sr., Little Nordside Press, 2002

Virgin Islands, George T. Eggleston, D. Van Nostrand Company, Inc., 1959, 1973 (Krieger Publishing, revised reprint)

Virgin Islands National Park website at *http://www.nps.gov.viis*

Virgin Islands, Report of Joint Commission of Congress, January 20, 1920, Washington, Government Printing Office

"Where's the Best Snorkeling?" National Park Service, publication date and printing source unknown

Wikipedia and Wikimedia Websites

Text Credits
Credits for quoted text sources are indicated in the text immediately following each quoted source. We also acknowledge extensive use of research.

Photograph and Illustration Credits
Credits for photographs and illustrations are indicated below each item. Principal credited sources were *Wikipedia, Wikimedia,* and the **Virgin Island National Park Service**.

A Special Thanks! for help and guidance provided by
Bill Kossler, editor, *The Source* (*St. Thomas, St. John,* and *St. Croix*) for permission to use information from articles that appeared in this newspaper; **Bish Denham** and **Boulon family members** for their help with information they provided related to Erva Boulon; **Aimery Caron**, professor emeritus, University of the Virgin Islands for permission to use his translations and for assistance with information related to his family and their historical ties to the Virgin Islands and St. John; **Doris and Ivan Jadan family members** (especially **Leslie Paoletti** and **Clay Hiles**) for their help with pulling together stories and memories about Doris and Ivan; **Eleanor Gibney**, long-time St. John resident and past president

SOURCES AND CREDITS   **223**

of the St. John Historical Society for permission to include a quotation from her mother's article, "Finding Out Different," and for taking the time to help us better understand the genesis of the Gibney-Oppenheimer property; **Damaris Botwick** and her daughter **Fiona Botwick** for permission to include information from *St. John Voices* and *St. John Backtime*, written and complied by Damaris's mother and Fiona's grandmother, Ruth Hull Low; **David. W. Knight, Sr.**, Director of Danish West Indies Research, Virgin Islands Historical & Genealogical Center for use of his published information about Annaberg and other historic references; historian **Leif Calundann Larsen**, Institute of History, Copenhagen University for use of information published in *The Danish Colonization of St. John 1718-1733;* **Marla Hood** of Cengage and **Ann Krieger** of Krieger Publishing for help with identification of copyright holder of George T. Eggleston's 1959 publication *Virgin Islands;* for assistance, support, and permissions provided by **members of the Eggleston family** (especially **Beth** and **George Pierson**); **Lonnie Willis**, president of the St. John Historical Society for help and guidance with contacting authors whose works were critical to this publication; a huge thanks to Danish author and researcher **Jens Ole Ravn-Nielsen** for his patience, insights, and guidance with our understanding of Countess Daisy and her story; **MaLinda Nelson**, publisher/editor of *St. John Magazine* for the years spent publishing this valuable, high quality magazine, which provided numerous articles that were of great assistance in writing this guidebook; the publisher of *Harper's Magazine* for special permission to include an excerpt about the Reef Bay Estate House by Paul Brooks, which was reproduced from the December 1960 issue of the magazine; and a round of thanks to our friend **Nick Nobbe** for his invaluable editorial assistance.

An extra special note of thanks goes to the V. I. National Park Service for the valuable informational materials provided through its brochures, pamphlets, plaques, and park website.

My Island Ways
A nonprofit corporation,
organized for educational purposes.